FACE THE CAMERA

THE PORTRAIT PHOTOGRAPHY OF

JOHN PHILPOTT

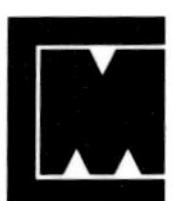

CREATIVE MONOCHROME
CONTEMPORARY PORTFOLIO SERIES

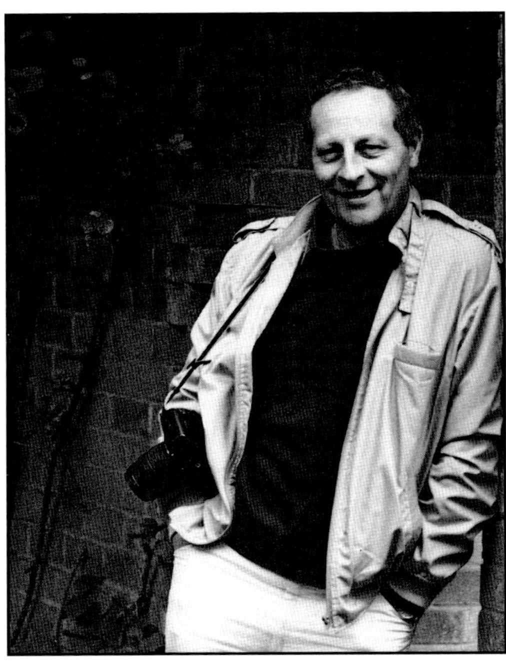

Photograph by Joan Wakelin, Hon FRPS

JOHN J PHILPOTT MBE FRPS was, for ten years, the in-house photographer for Ordnance Survey. During this time, he photographed several members of the Royal Family and many other eminent people. He was a founder and life member of the OS Photographic Society and was awarded the MBE for his services to Ordnance Survey. Although he retired from OS in 1991, he was asked back to photograph the special events of its 200th anniversary year, including the visit of the Queen and Prince Philip to the historical exhibition at the Tower of London.

John is a Fellow of the Royal Photographic Society, having gained this distinction with a panel of images which was described by Joan Wakelin in *The Photographic Journal* as being of "stunning quality". His work has been widely exhibited and has received awards in several national and international photographic competitions and exhibitions.

FACE THE CAMERA
The portrait photography of
JOHN J PHILPOTT MBE FRPS

Published in the UK by Creative Monochrome
20 St Peters Road, Croydon, Surrey, CR0 1HD.

British Library Cataloguing-in-Publication Data:
A catalogue record for this book is available from the British Library

ISBN 1 873319 12 6
First edition, 1994

Printed in England by Butler & Tanner Ltd,
Caxton Road, Frome, Somerset.

Foreword

Tony Worobiec FRPS

The act of taking a portrait is one of the most common photographic activities known to man. Indeed, the whole of the photographic industry is geared up to acknowledge this: cameras and lenses are designed to aid portraiture, and film emulsions and printing papers are precisely balanced to best replicate the colour and tones of the human face. And yet as commonplace as this activity is, there are precious few photographers who can make consistently good portraits.

Why should this be? While most of us are quite content to be photographed by one of our nearest or dearest, the notion that somebody less familiar should take our 'portrait' is generally considered threatening. Unless the photographer has very special social skills and is immediately able to put people at their ease, that inapprehensible aura which is so subtly expressed through facial and bodily gesticulations, and which is unique to each individual, is lost. In this case, the photograph becomes a lifeless record: it has body but no soul.

John Philpott is, in my opinion, a very special photographer. He has a vitally important gift: a wonderful capacity to empathise. Like a good writer, a good portraitist needs to be a shrewd observer, rapidly evaluating changing moods and expressions, but remaining ever vigilant that the sitter does not feel intimidated. All the photographs in this book show a master in control.

John does not deal in stolen images. He seeks, almost without exception, to establish camera to eye contact, because it is only in this way that the true character of the subject can be revealed. He recognises and uses the power of the eyes to communicate feelings and has the expertise and understanding to react precisely at the moment when the eye is at its most revealing. The myriad of emotions captured in this stimulating portfolio range from humour to thoughtfulness, and from candour to introspection; and yet all convey conviction and a genuine sense of humanity.

I was especially drawn to the image of the old tramp in the darkened alleyway – the harshness of his present existence so clearly etched about his face. The opportunity for the usual tramp clichés abounds (and haven't we seen enough of them?), but in this instance one senses that the photographer has not only won the trust of the old man, but genuinely cares for him. I can imagine John engaging the old man in conversation. The tramp is about to reveal aspects of his life nobody has cared to listen to for years. It is an image which deliberately seeks to express feelings. Note how the photographer has included the hand, aware of its importance in revealing the human psyche. On a subliminal level, it is interwoven with rich innuendo and stark visual messages which so characterise John Philpott's photography.

In preparing this foreword, it was a wonderful experience to talk with John about his approach to portraiture and how he comes by his sitters. Many he knows casually, either from work or people who live close to hand. He does not scour the streets looking for subjects, as if they were prime specimens, there only to advance his photographic career. How on earth can one empathise in such a predatorial fashion?

But John is equally capable of exploiting an opportunity when it presents itself. His wonderful portrait of the 'Octogenarian' arose from a chance meeting while walking through the woods. She engaged John in conversation, enquiring what he was looking for to photograph. She and the world knew that her face was deeply lined, but John saw deeper. He suggested taking her portrait and it seems that she trusted him immediately. Her instincts were right and her reward was a wonderfully revealing image showing pathos, yet nobility. While age has undoubtedly taken its toll, she is presented as an assertive and independent lady.

John is an extremely fine printer, recognising that the mood and character of his sitters can best be conveyed through the careful manipulation of tone. His decision to work exclusively in monochrome was an obvious one, but his recurring emphasis on low-key tonality has proved inspirational. The faces he shows us glow against sombre backgrounds, which John is careful never to allow to become too intrusive. He undoubtedly knows his craft and is able to 'punctuate' the final print with all the tonal modulation reminiscent of his avowed hero, Karsh of Ottowa.

John Philpott is undeniably a formidable technician. Some of these images are montages, while others rely on the exacting process of multiple printing for their ultimate success: and yet they are not in any way obvious – surely the hallmark of a highly skilled craftsman.

Underpinning all John's work is a superb sense of composition, which is so highly reliant on balance. He achieves this in many ways. His preferred option is to use tone, frequently employing a carefully chosen illuminated area in the background to counterbalance the strongly lit portrait. But he also achieves this desire for equilibrium in other ways, through framing or the clever use of the hands.

John hardly ever uses studio lighting and props, preferring instead to use the sitter's own environment. Whilst this undoubtedly helps to put his subjects at their ease, it nevertheless creates problems for the photographer. John, however, translates such problems into fresh compositional opportunities, preventing his work from ever appearing formulaic.

The human physiognomy is a particularly compelling subject for many serious photographers, not so much for what it tells us of the sitter, but rather for what it tells us of ourselves. Images with this level of insight invite the viewer to relate to them directly, recognising their own fears and frailties, their own hopes and aspirations.

John Philpott has presented an intriguing portfolio of work, which displays originality, wit and incisiveness, but above all, humanity.

TONY WOROBIEC FRPS is the Head of Design at Purbeck School, Dorset. He is a member of the Arena group of photographers and of the Royal Photographic Society's Associateship and Fellowship distinctions panels for visual arts.

INTRODUCTION

JOHN J PHILPOTT MBE FRPS

Nature has been very generous to portrait photographers, providing subject matter which is infinitely diverse and limitless in supply.

The great joy of photography – whether it is landscape, natural history, pictorial or portrait – is the individual interpretation of the subject. I like to think that every time I take a picture of someone, it is a completely unique work. Any other photographer of the same subject would create a quite different picture.

Such differences arise from a number of factors. Some, such as choice of cameras, lenses, lighting and printing techniques, are primarily technical, while others are more a matter of personal style. The personality of the photographer, for example, will cause different emotions to emerge from the subject. Even our height and shape influence the angles from which we shoot. I believe that everything that has happened to you in life influences the selection, framing and composition of the pictures you take from the day you pick up your first camera and go looking for a subject.

Throughout my life as a photographer, I'm conscious of having been influenced by many different factors, but the thread which runs consistently through the years and which has made the greatest impact on my work is the camera club. I cherish the pleasure of sharing skills and experiences with other enthusiasts at club meetings and the excitement of battle in competitions and exhibitions. Some of the more celebrated practitioners may belittle such simple pleasures, but then they have their own platforms.

I have spent many a happy evening at amateur club gatherings listening to lectures and looking at photographs. I owe a debt to many photographers around the club circuit who have encouraged me and helped me to progress. Two, in particular, who have been a significant influence are Chris Wainwright and Joan Wakelin.

I was very lucky in my early club days to have seen, on two occasions, Karl Pollack. He was a truly great portraitist, very similar to Karsh in style and, in my opinion, as good. I am grateful that I was able to see his work so early in my photographic life and to be set such a great example of attention to detail, lighting, subject selection, and print quality.

What a wonderful character. I have fond memories of his beret and black shirt, his mid-European accent and his infectious enthusiasm. I remember him, during one of his lectures, clutching a print to his chest as if he could not bear to be parted from it. You could feel the sense of anticipation in the audience. He told the story of a woman who came to his studio and asked what he would charge for a postcard. "Postcard?" – his voice thundered with incredulity. And then he saw the subject: a ragged little black boy with big, luminous eyes; he was wearing braces to hitch his short trousers, from which half the buttons were missing. "Madam," he said, "you can have all ze postcards you vant". Then, with the timing and flourish of a great showman, he banged the resulting print up on the board with a cry of exultation.

One of the most enjoyable aspects of camera club life is the variety of characters you meet. In the early days of the Ordnance Survey Photographic Society, we had a secretary who made an excellent job of running the club, even though he didn't own a camera. Committee meetings were very much a one-man show, and it was a brave man who would interrupt or gainsay this formidable character.

The day came when one of the members reported that he was able to get a model willing to do figure work. Now this was the late 'fifties: some of us had only heard rumours of what girls looked like between chin and ankles. There was a breathless hush as all eyes turned instinctively to the 'Hon. Sec.' for his reaction. To break the silence, someone suggested limiting the meeting to only eight people – and genuine photographers at that.

After much wobbling of the Adam's apple, the secretary agreed, on condition that only the dedicated few would be invited. On the big day, no-one passed comment when the secretary himself arrived, wielding a brand new camera and tripod.

What a fiasco that first session was. I took one film. When I developed it, I found that half of the images were portraits, and all of them spoilt by camera-shake! I have improved a little since those days, and now I find people asking me for advice on how to go about making effective portraits. My view is that you have to be true to yourself: make mistakes, find out how to avoid them, and discover what works for you. By all means be guided by and learn from other people, but pursue your own ideas.

The most common failing I find is that people are more concerned with the technicalities than the really important elements. When a fellow club member wanted to learn about portrait work, I set up the lights, lent him my tripod, coaxed the model into a relaxed mood, and told the aspiring portraitist to 'hit the button'. Instead of taking shots to win the next club competition, he turned round and asked if he should be at f/8 or f/11. The model has got lockjaw and I've got apoplexy, but Charlie boy still has his 36 shots left. You will never get pictures if you don't expose some film – the cheapest equipment in any photographer's camera bag.

The ability to communicate and put people at ease is an essential part of the portraitist's art. At a club portrait session, I watched someone taking pictures of a young girl. With his head bent over his twin lens reflex camera, he was mumbling instructions which the model was straining to hear. Suddenly he looked up and said, with all the imperious command he could muster, "Will you change your expression for the next shot, please?" Not a very promising pupil!

What is the right approach? It is different for each photographer, because it is so closely tied to the personality. I find that, quite subconsciously, I size up everyone I meet as a potential subject and every room I enter as a potential background. I try to visualise the person in the most appropriate situation. When working with a model, I keep chatting about what I am trying to achieve. I'm quite happy to make a fool of myself if that will help them to relax. I study their reactions to the things I say and observe their mannerisms and body language. After making the first exposure, I watch the sitter's face very carefully: having made a start, the tension goes from the face and I'm most likely to find the expression I'm looking for.

Some people come alive in front of a camera and, if the conditions are just right, you know there is a picture for the taking. The adrenalin begins to pump and the hair on the back of your neck bristles. The excitement is heightened by the knowledge of what can go wrong and that the opportunity may be lost forever. You are pitting your experience and expertise against such threats: raising your game to meet the challenges. This may sound over the top, but it's how it feels to me. And if the enthusiasm is there, then so is the magic.

DEDICATION

To my wife, Margaret,
for her constant love
and to our daughters, Jo and Vicky.

Portfolio

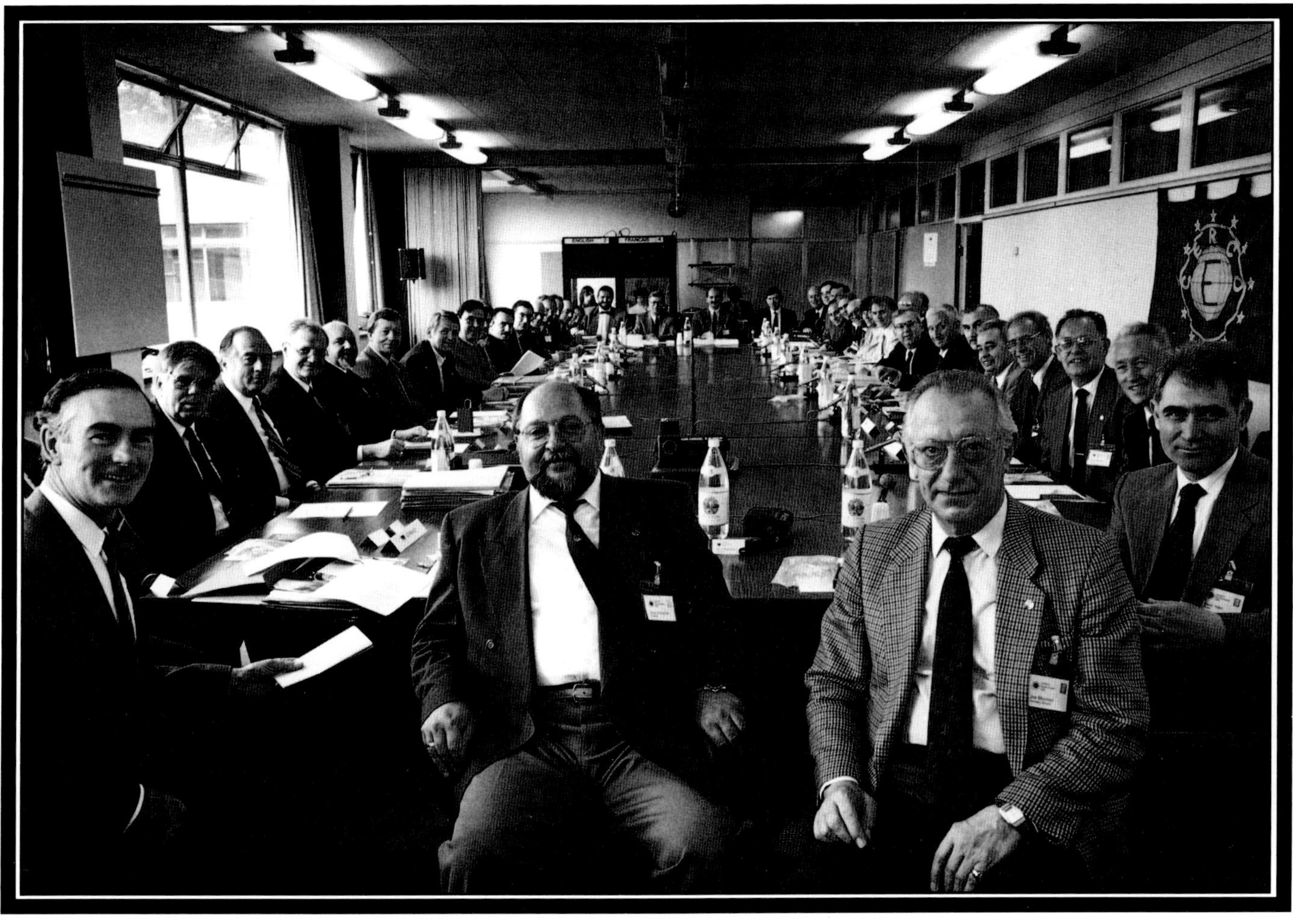

1.
Face the Camera
Ordnance Survey, 1991

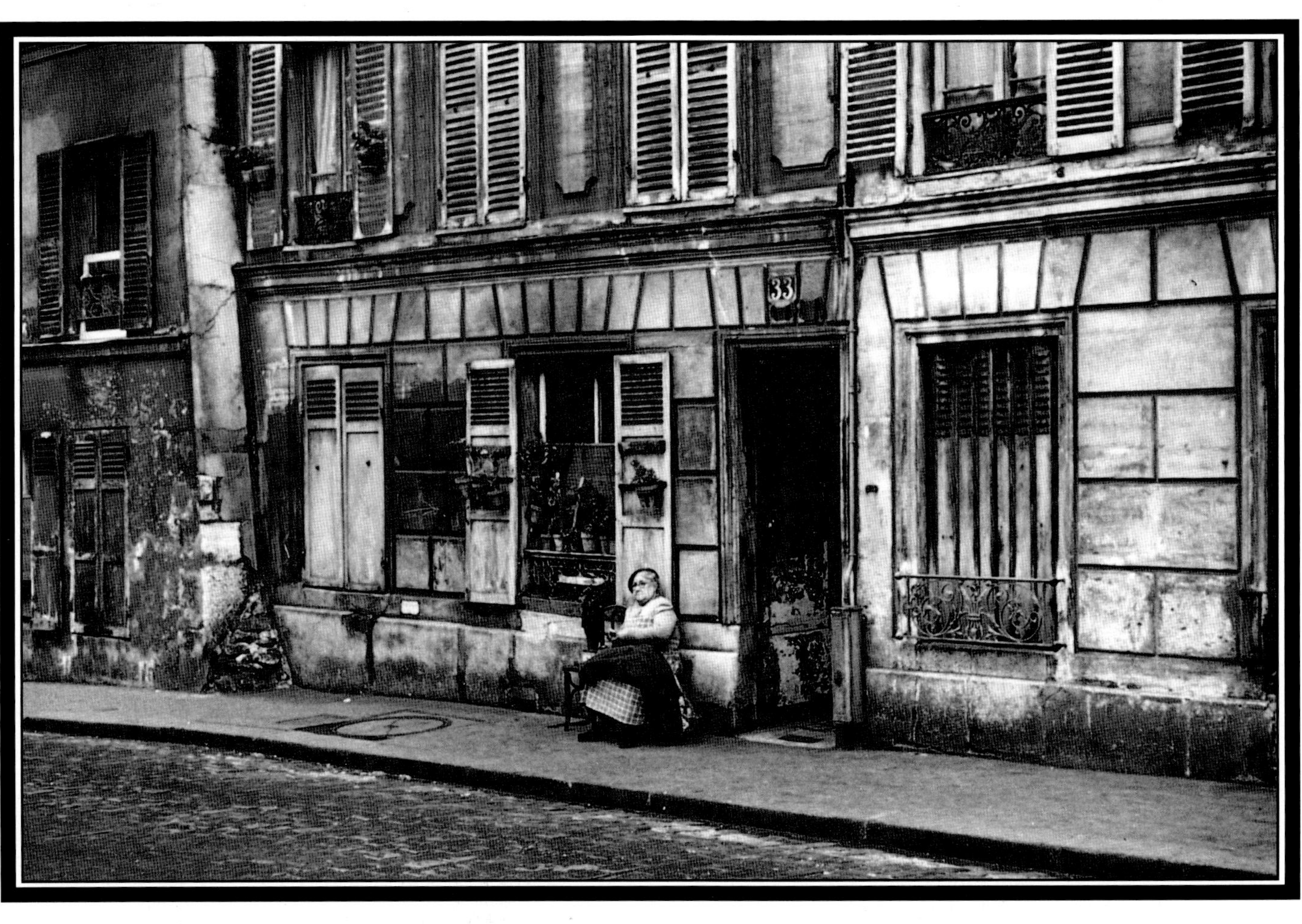

2.
Montmartre dwelling, No. 33

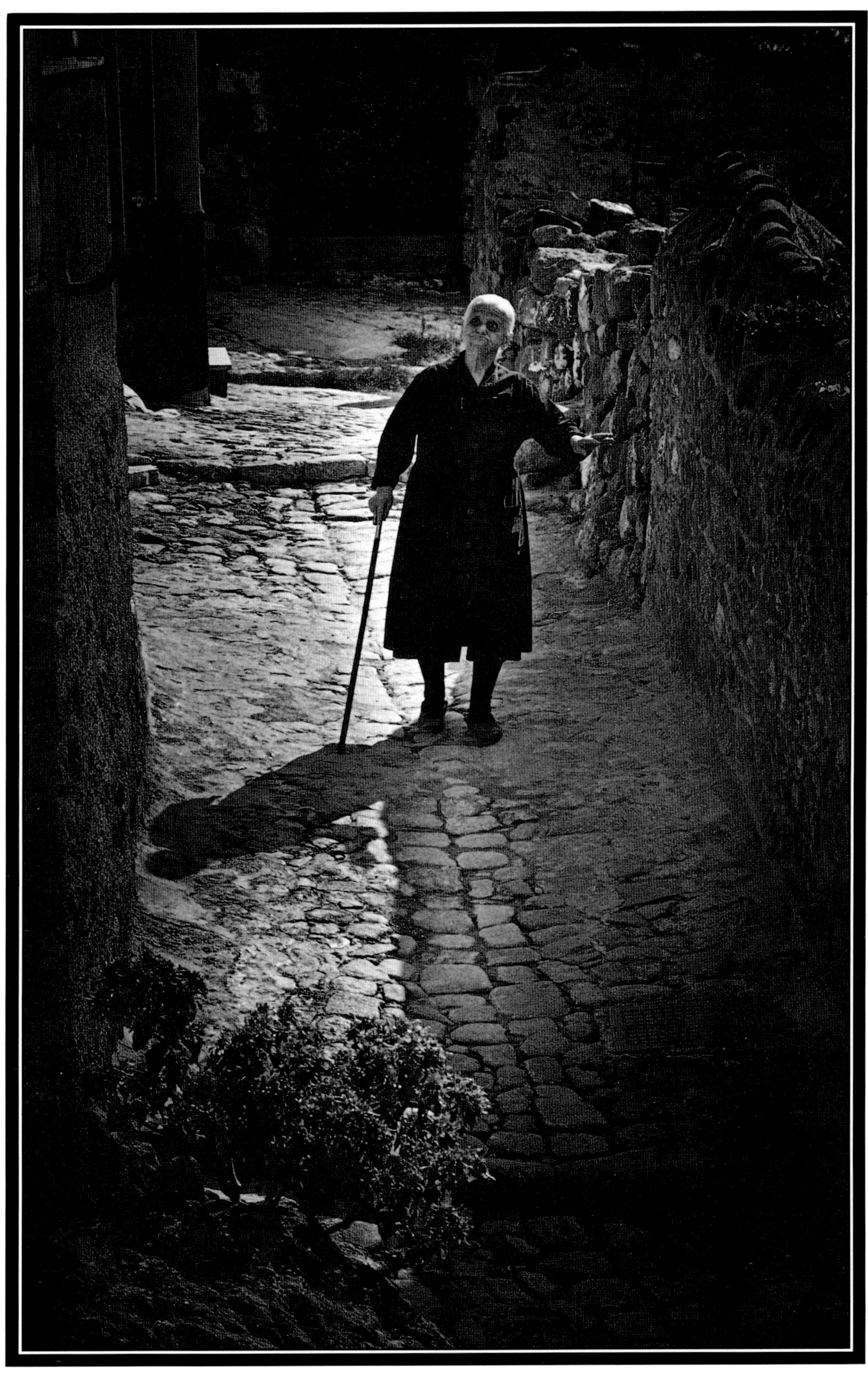

3.
Molyvos, 1987

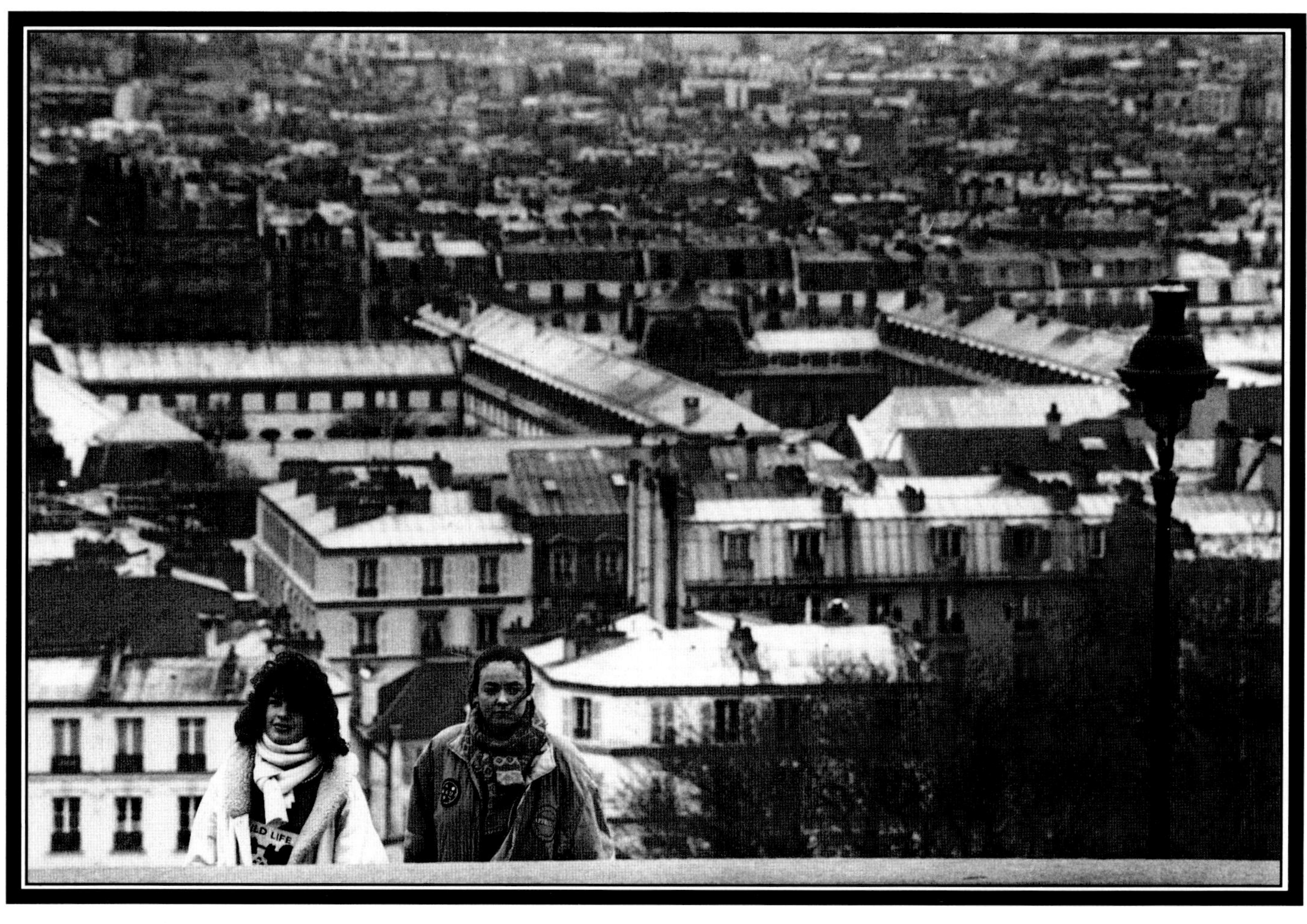

4.
Paris vista

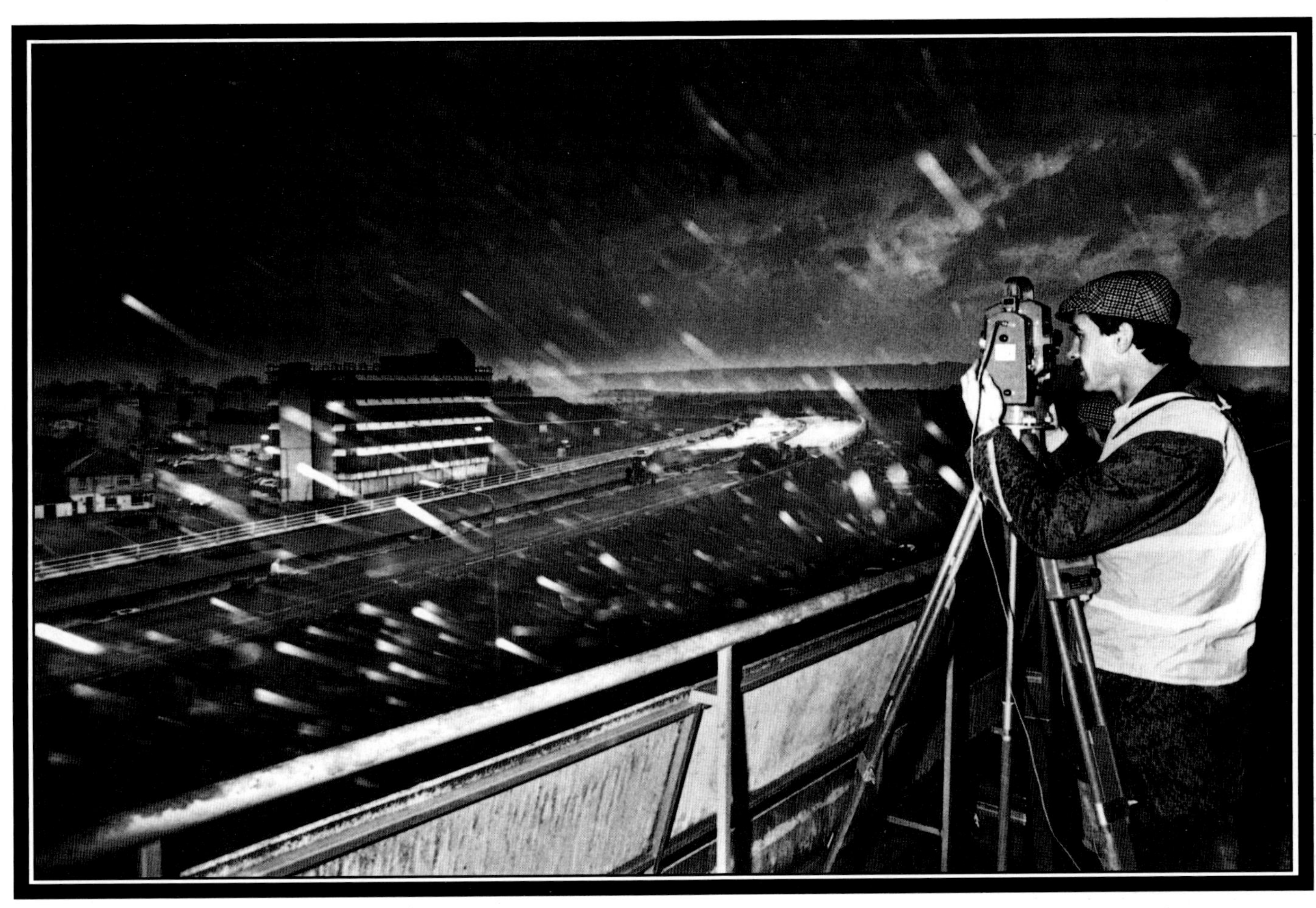

5.
OS Surveyor, 1988

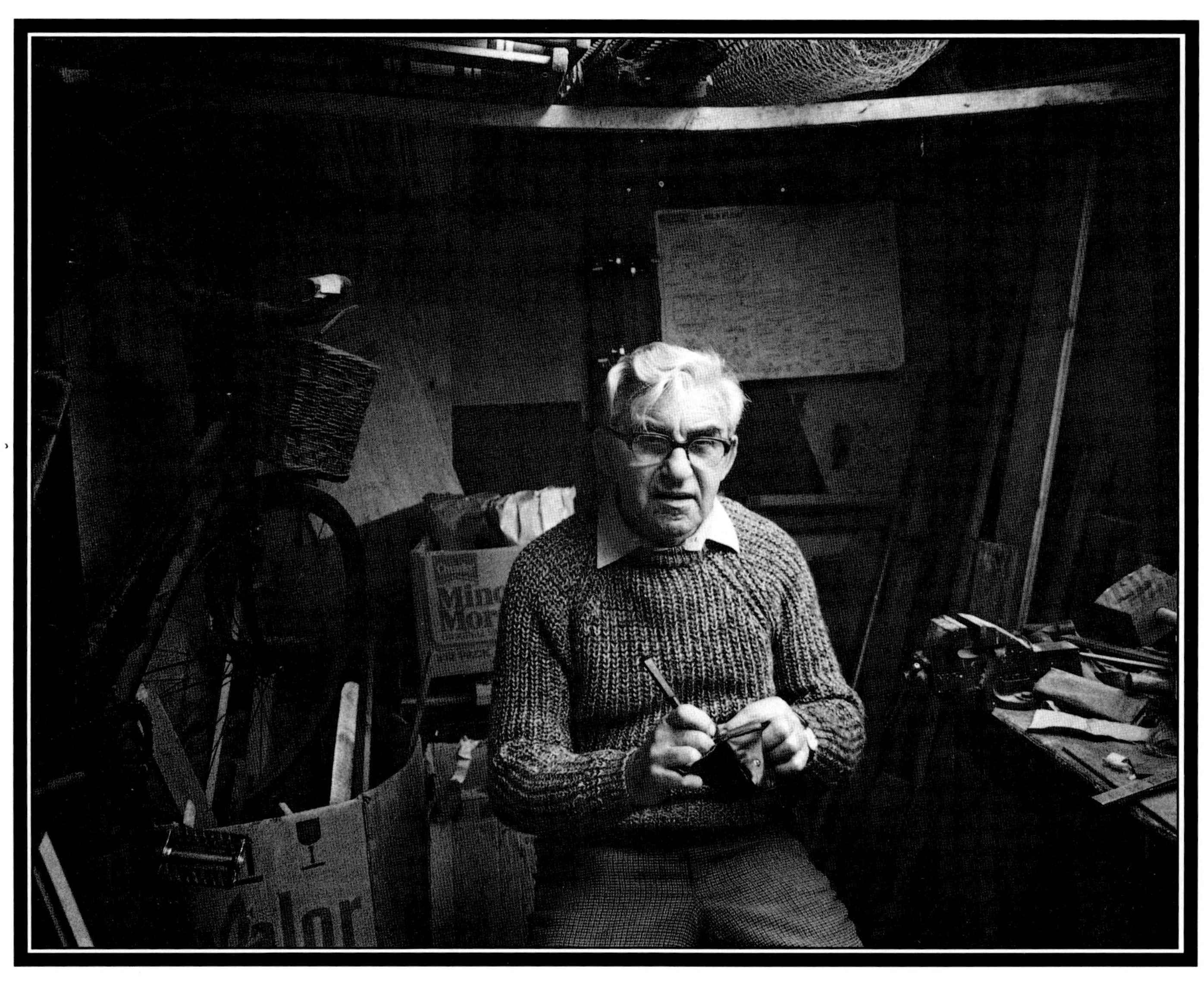

6.
Refuge

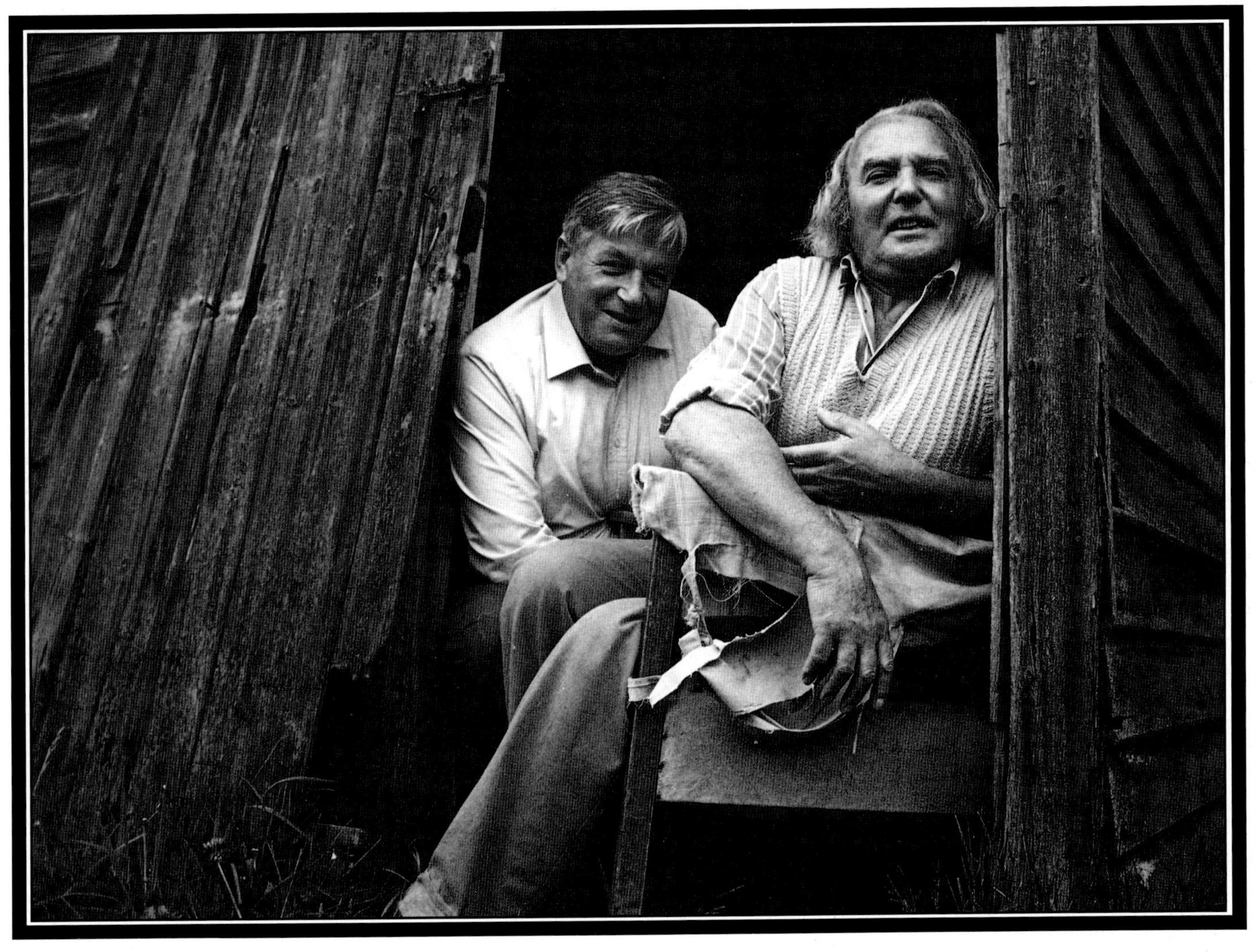

7.
Smile please

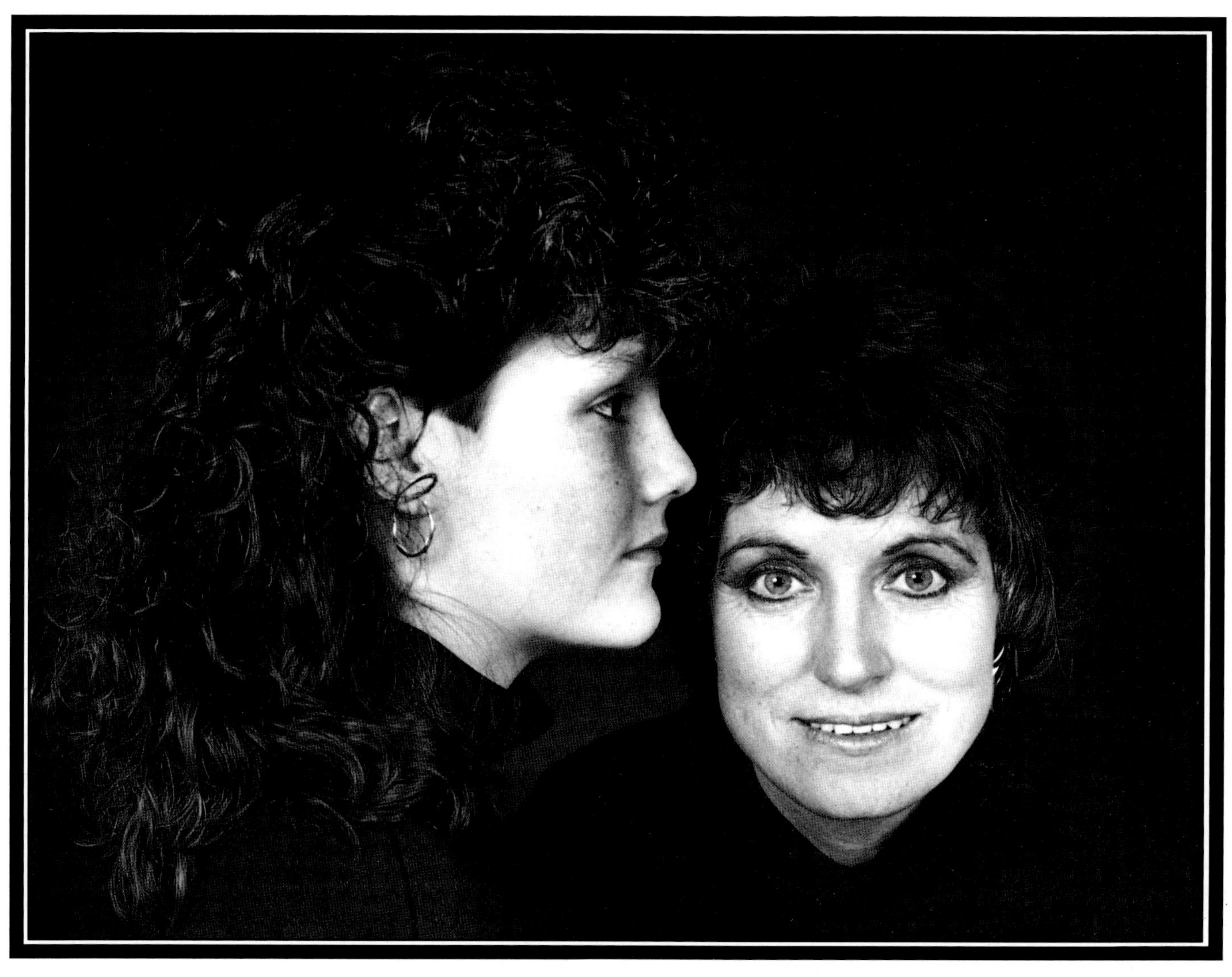

8.
Leha and daughter

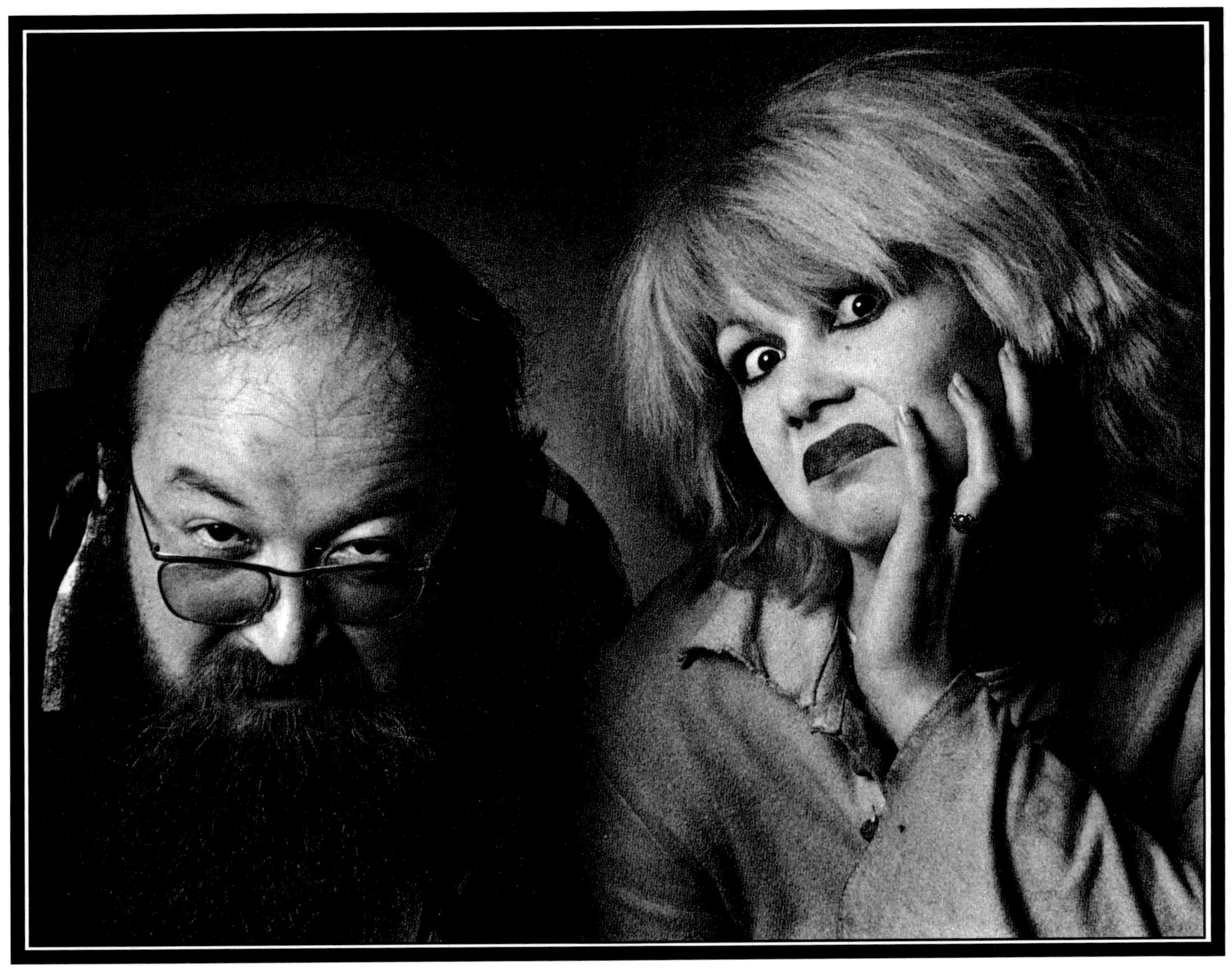

9.
He's not with me

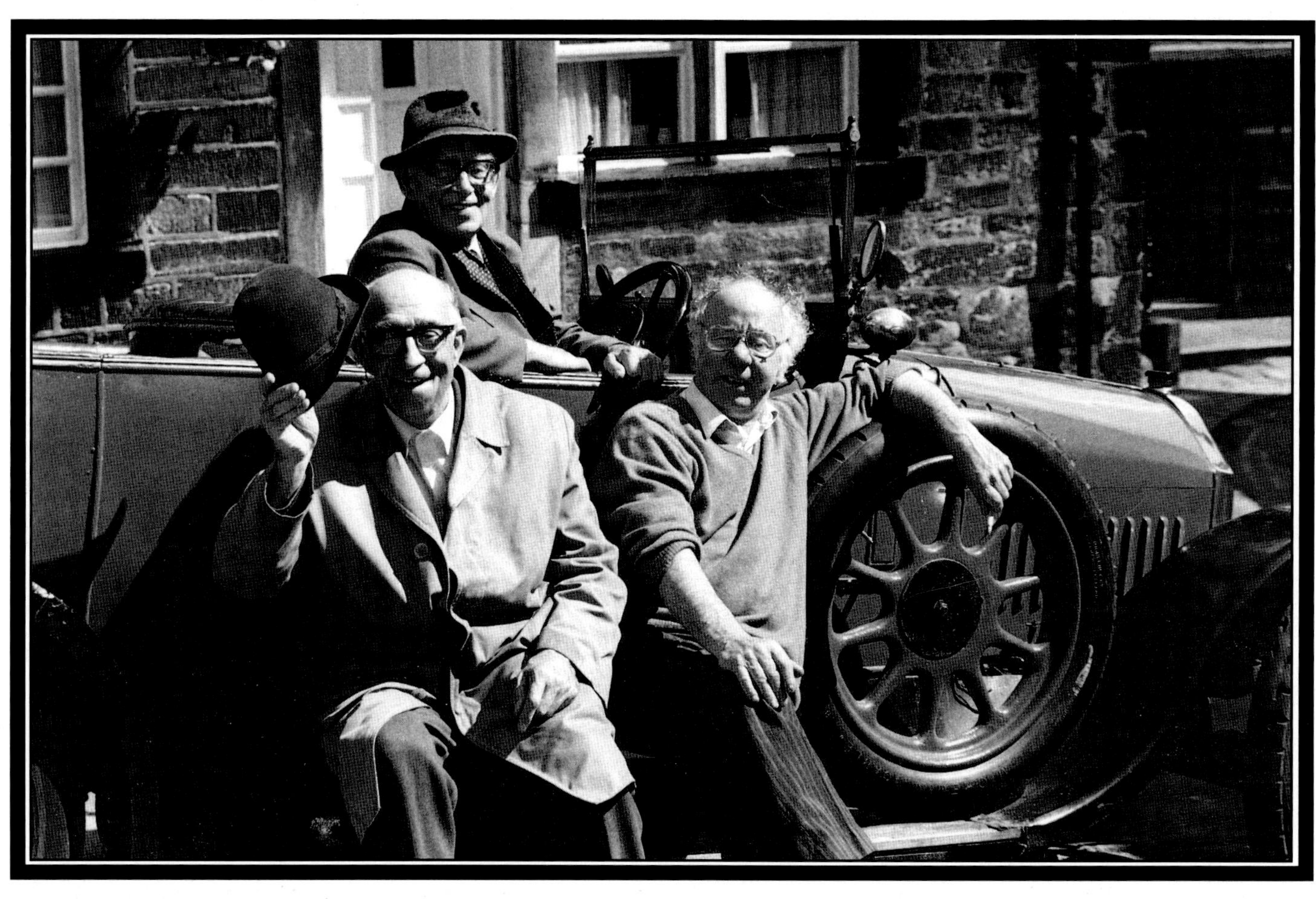

10.
Autumn leaves

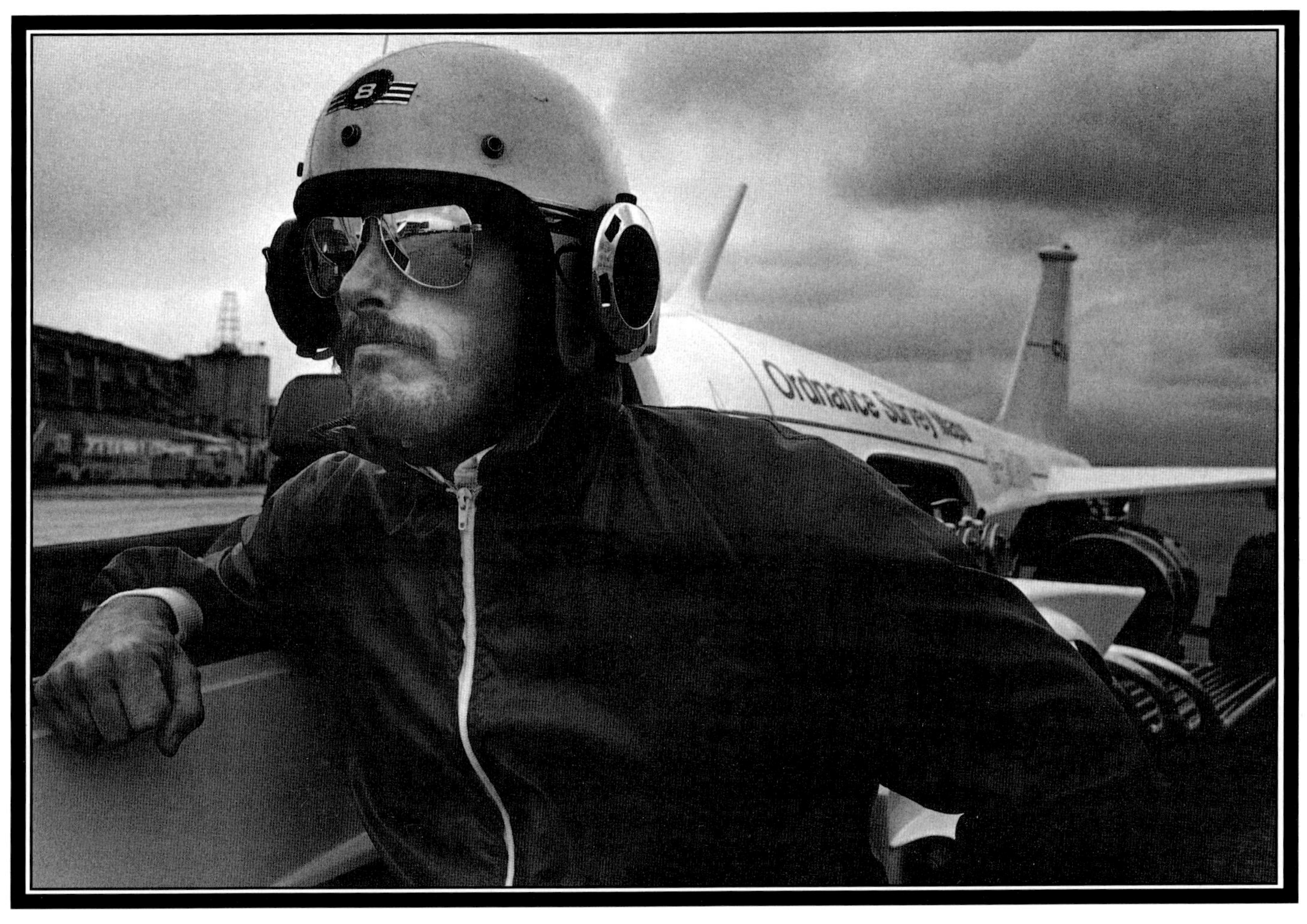

11.
The driver
Ordnance Survey, 1988

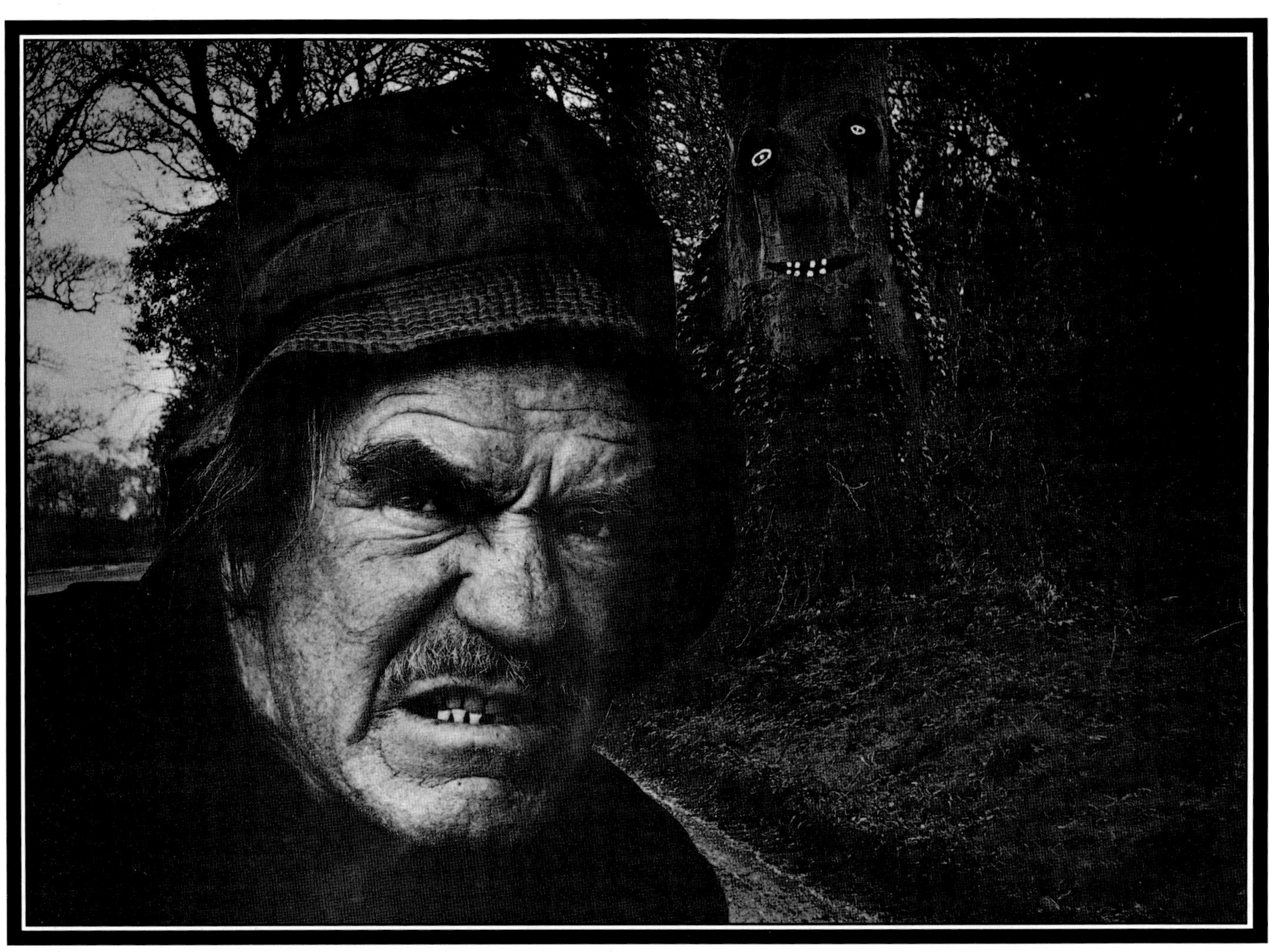

12.
Pals

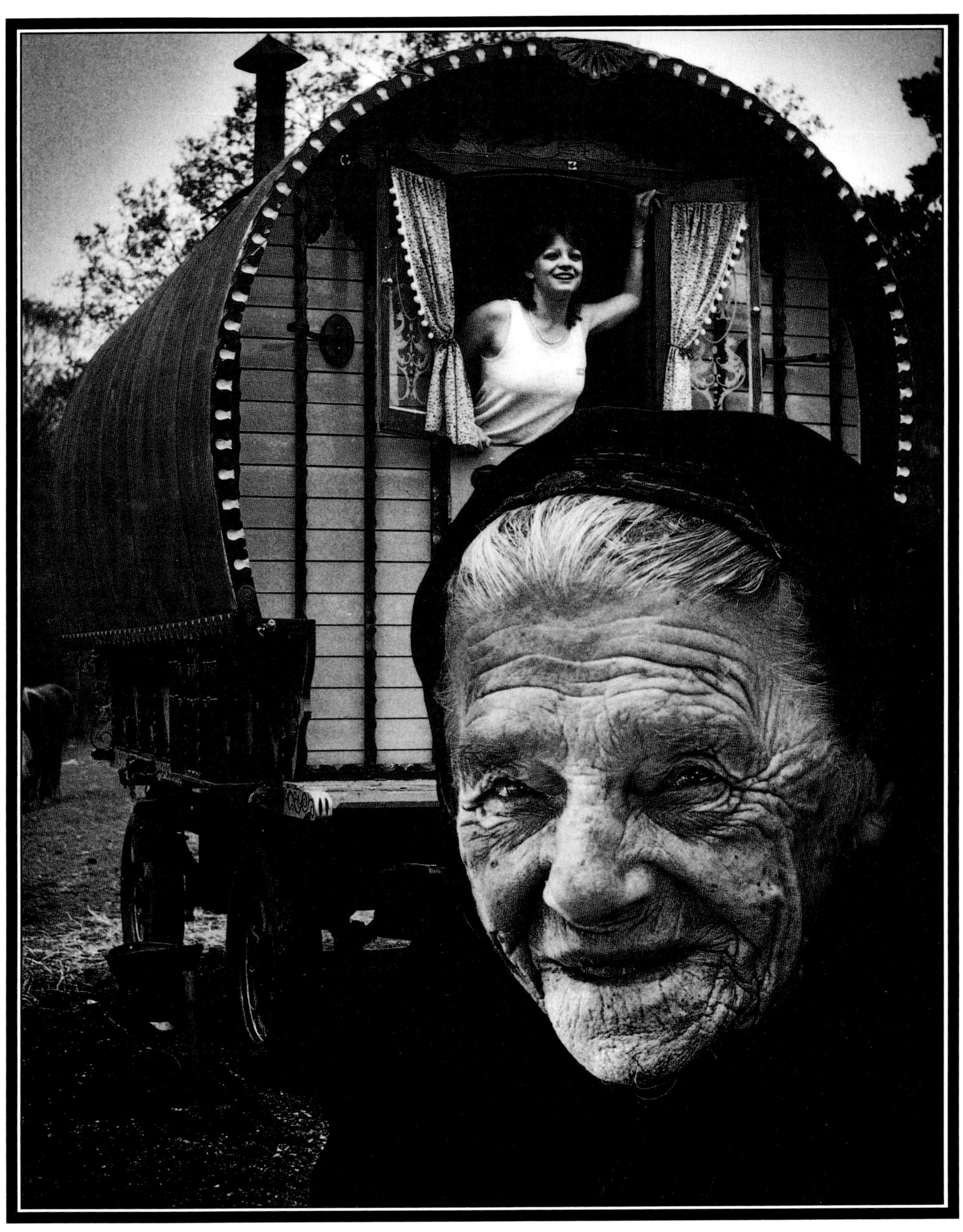

13.
"Tell yer fortune, luv?"

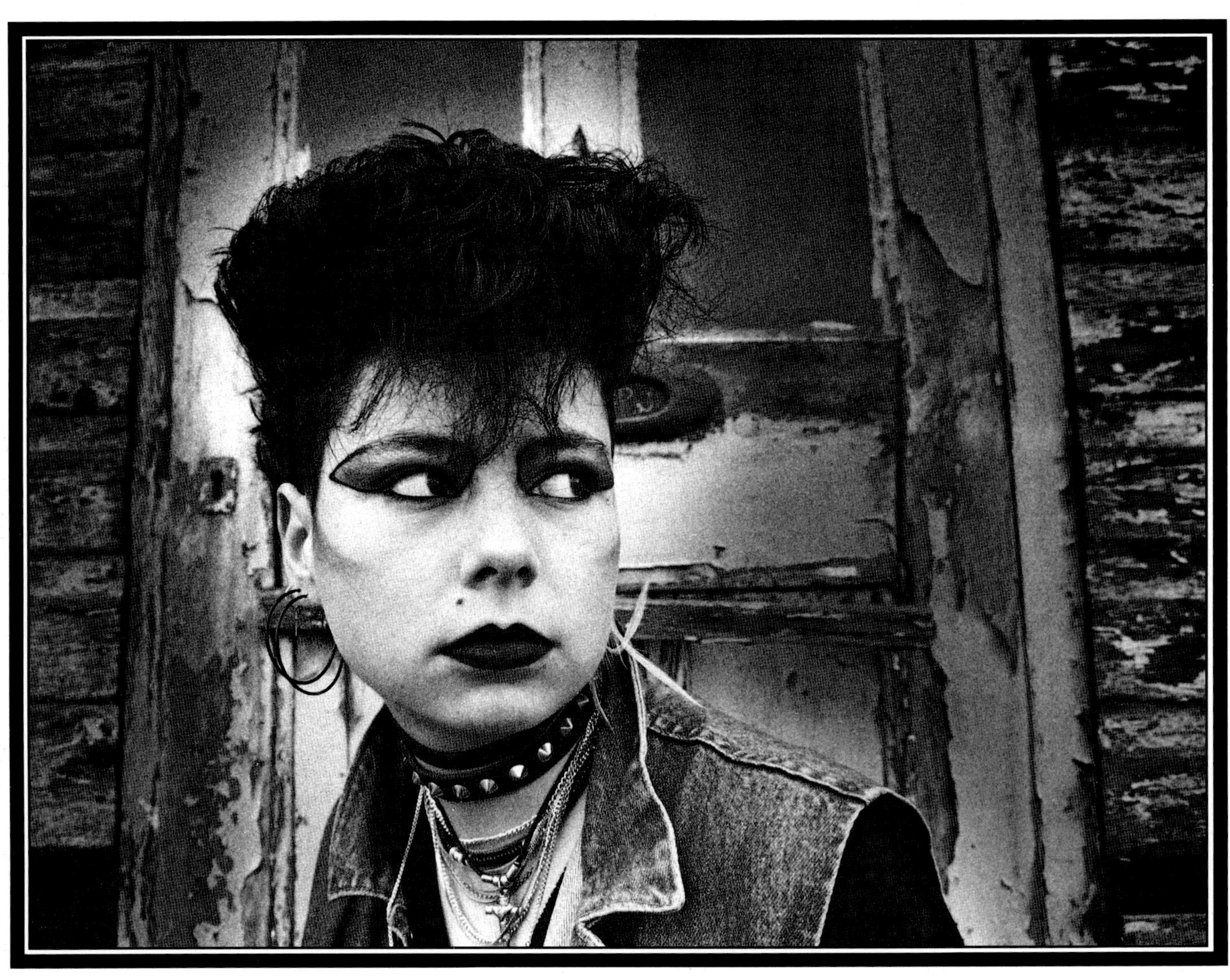

14.
Dressed up

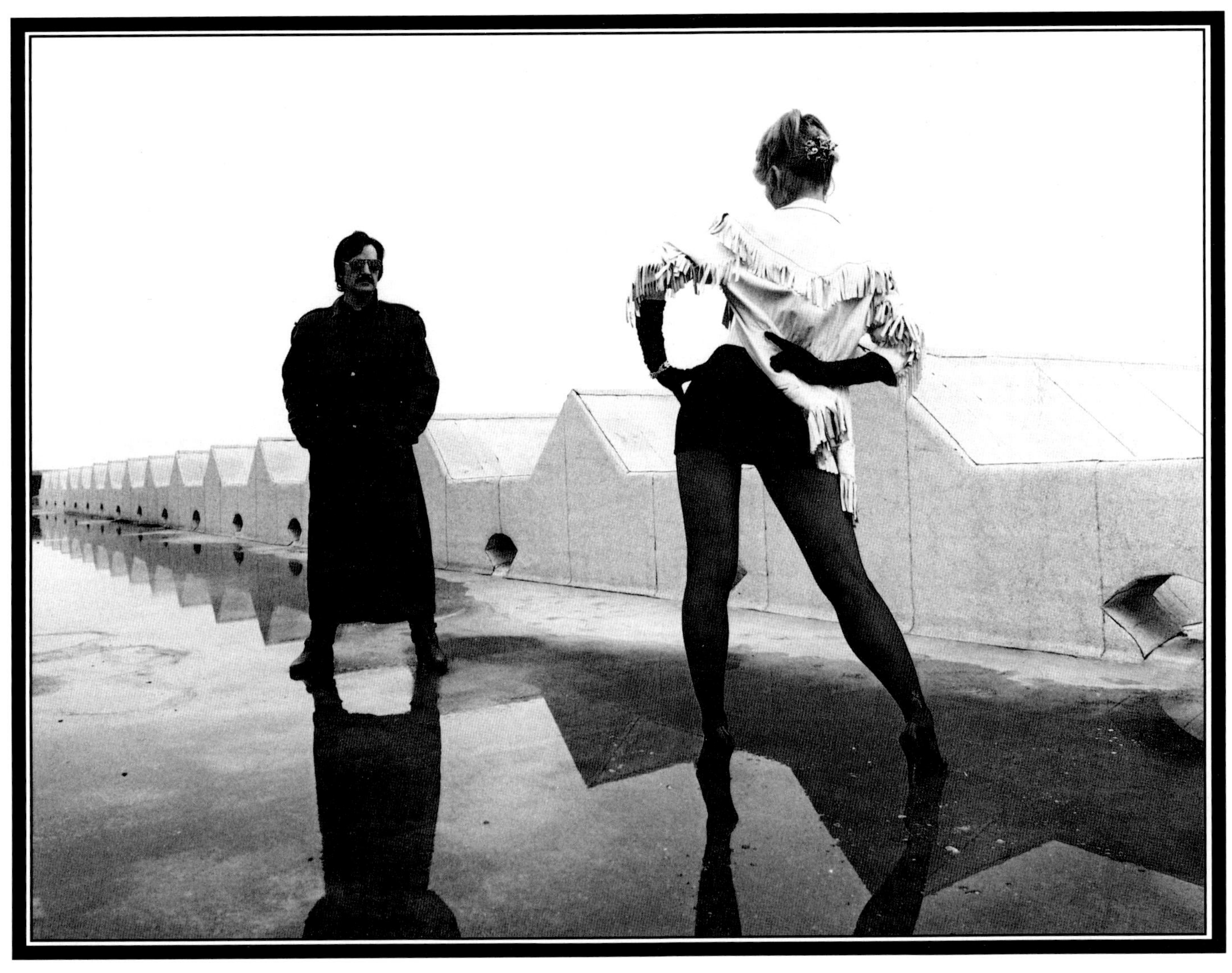

15.
Encounter

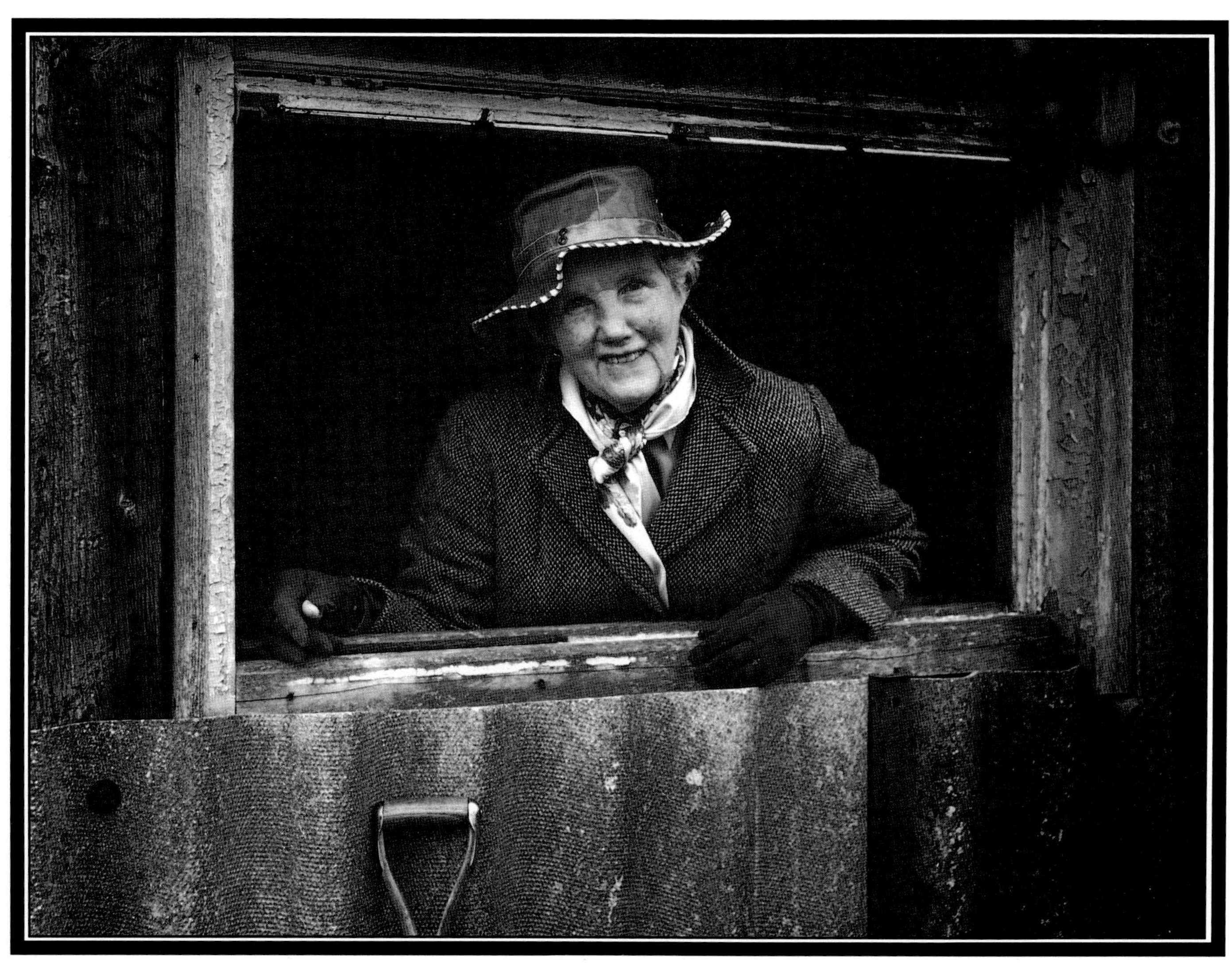

16.
Working lady

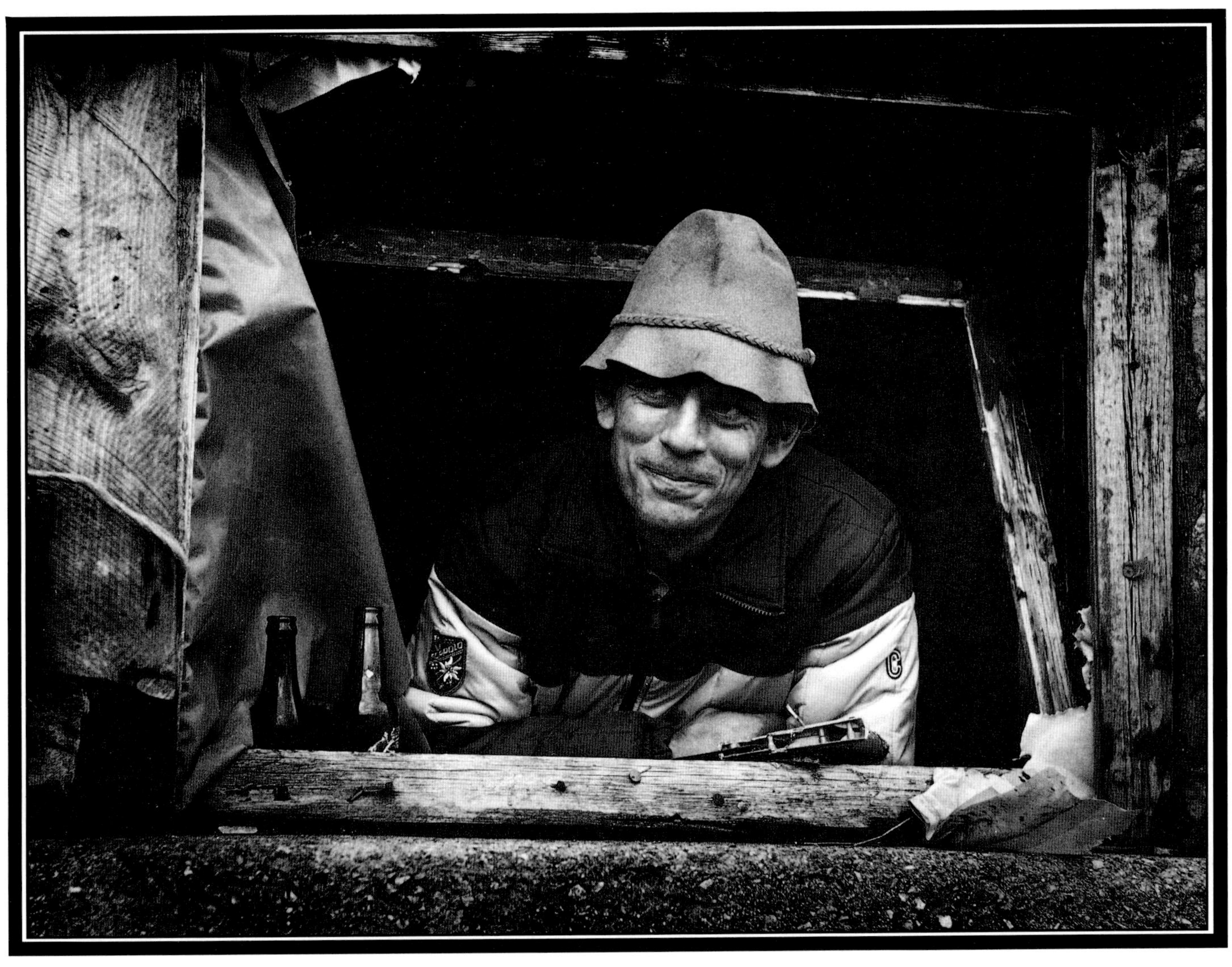

17.
Hide-away

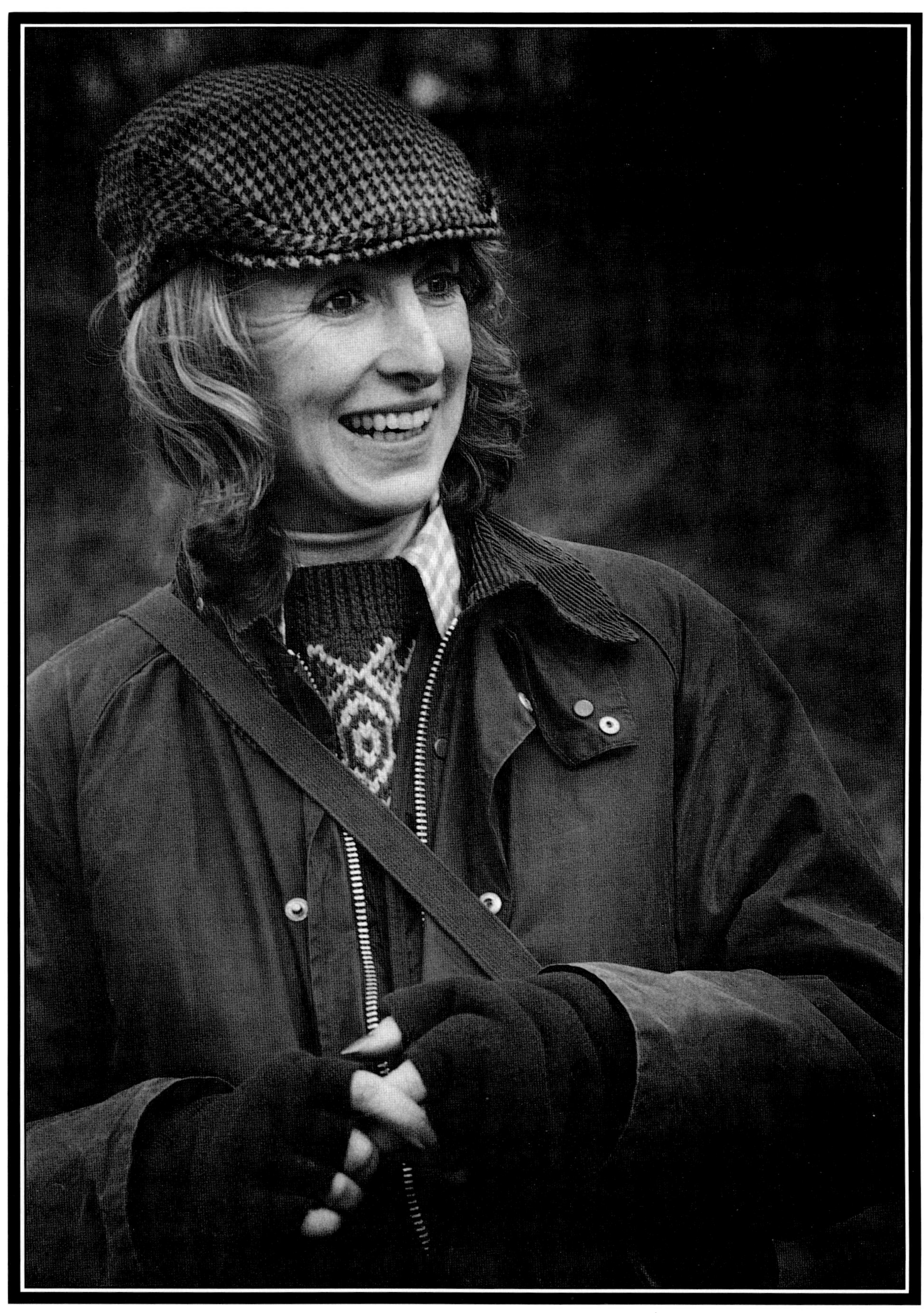

18.
O.K. yah?

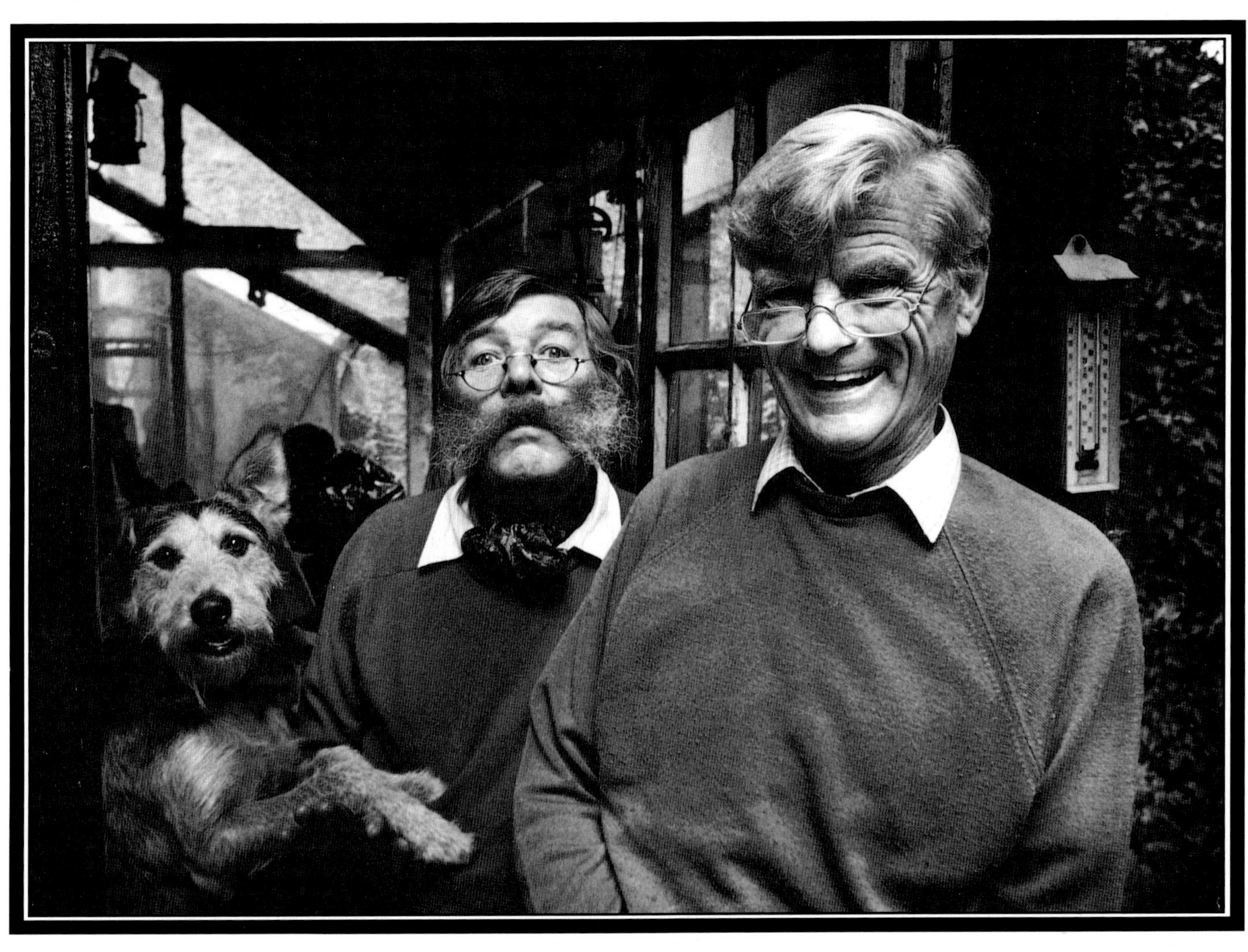

19.
Alan Chalmers and friends

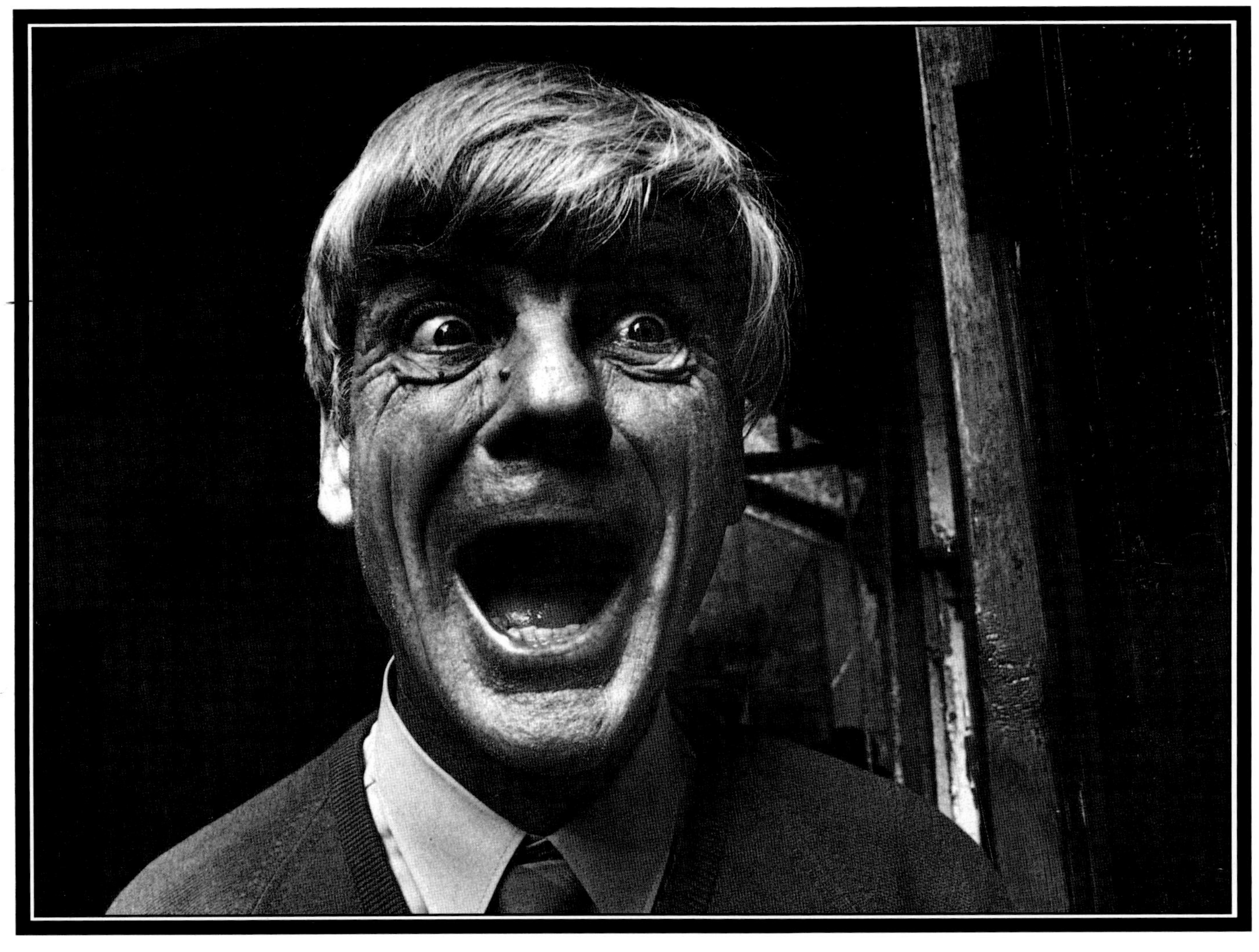

20.
Rodney Hurt
Life-long friend

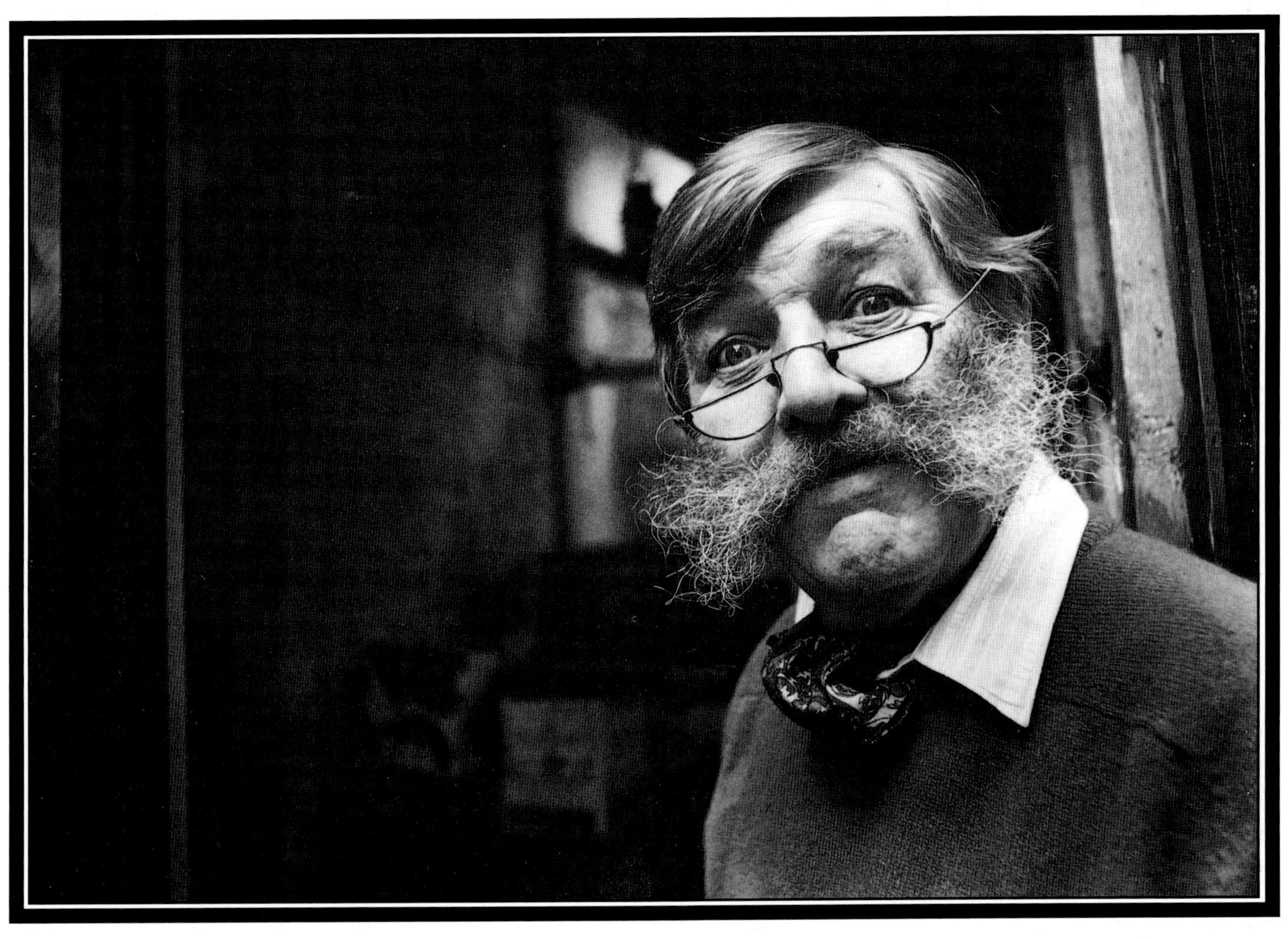

21.
Alan Chalmers
Life-long friend

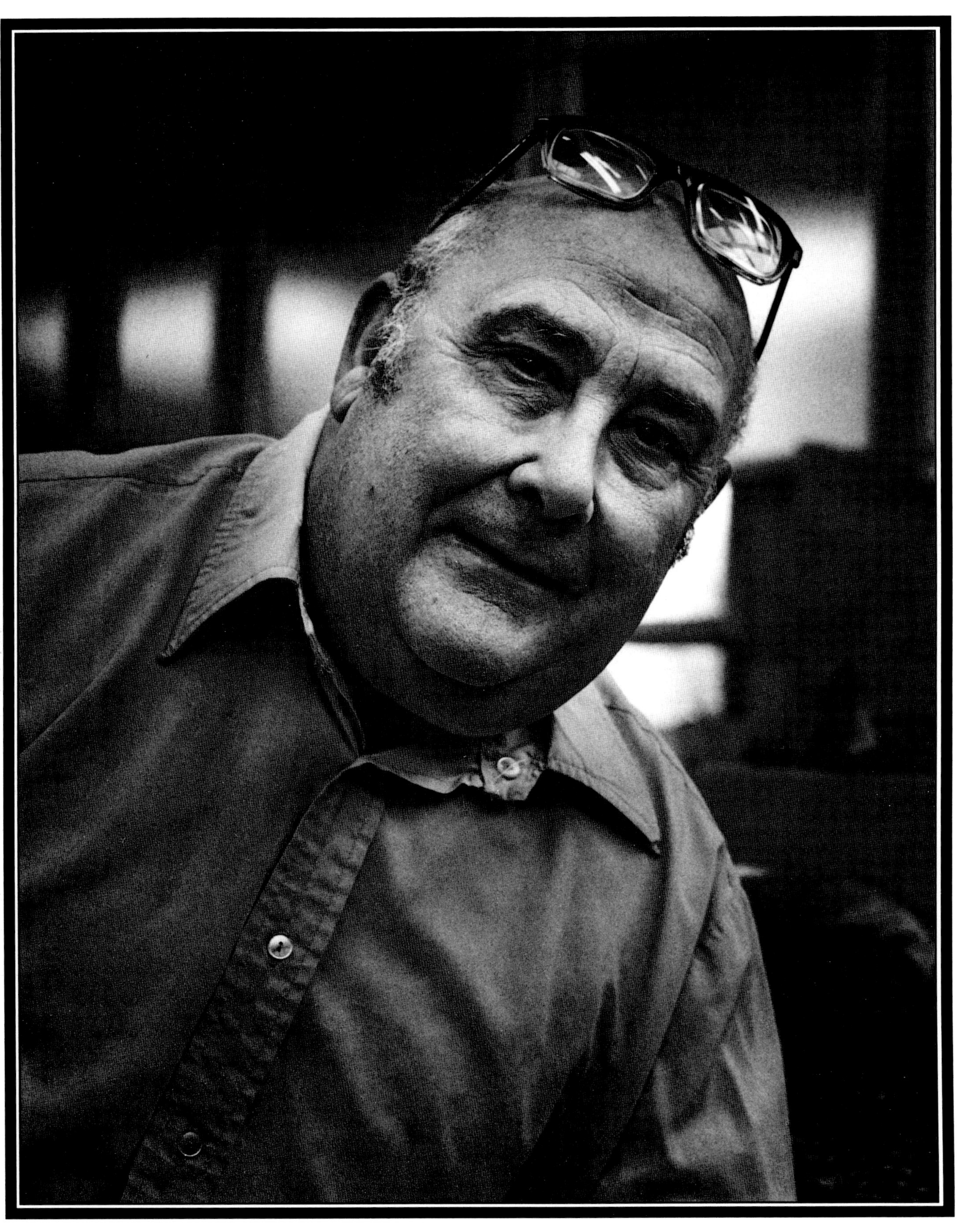

22.
Ray Olan
Ordnance Survey, 1986

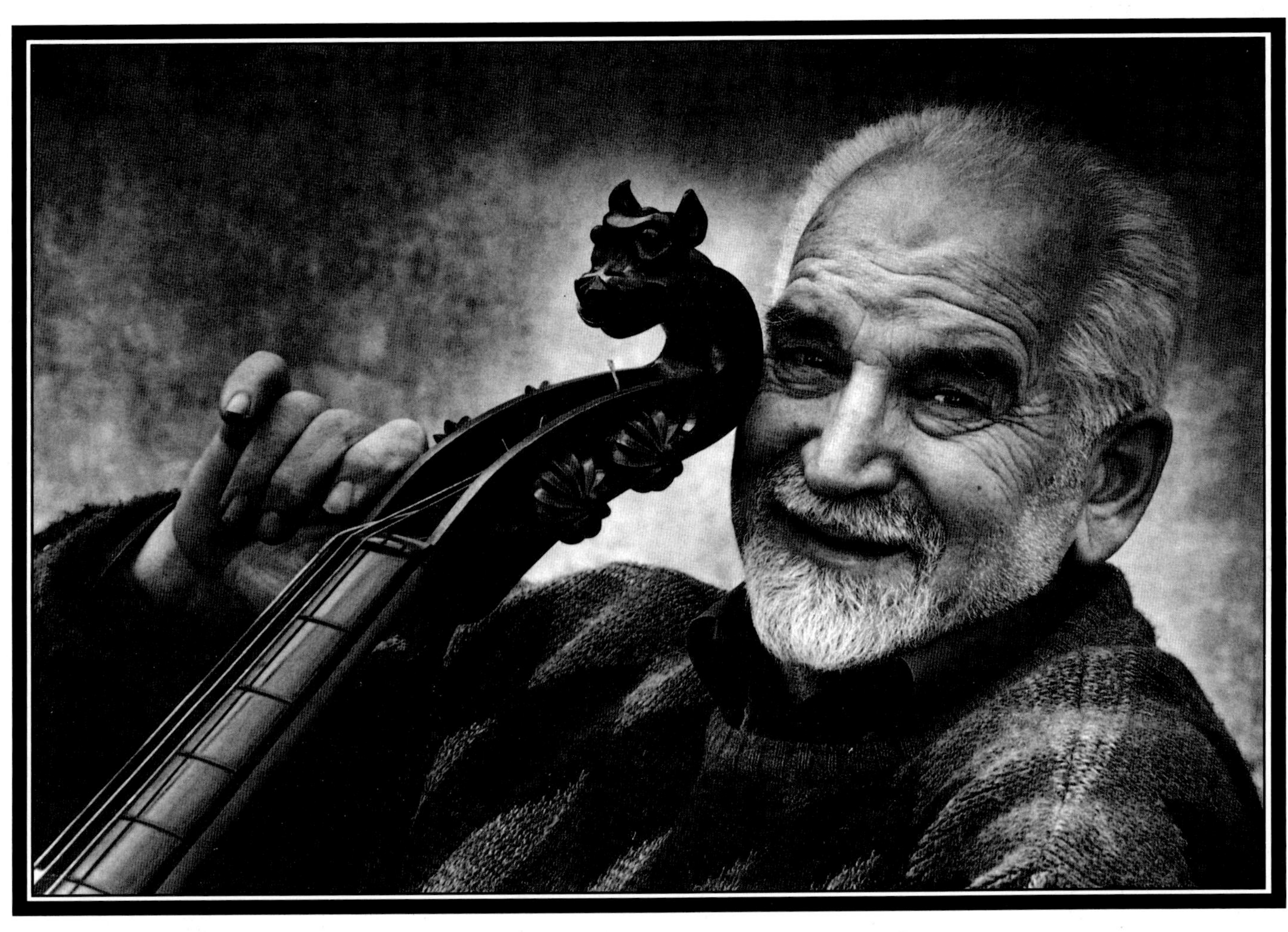

23.
Alex Oban
Musician

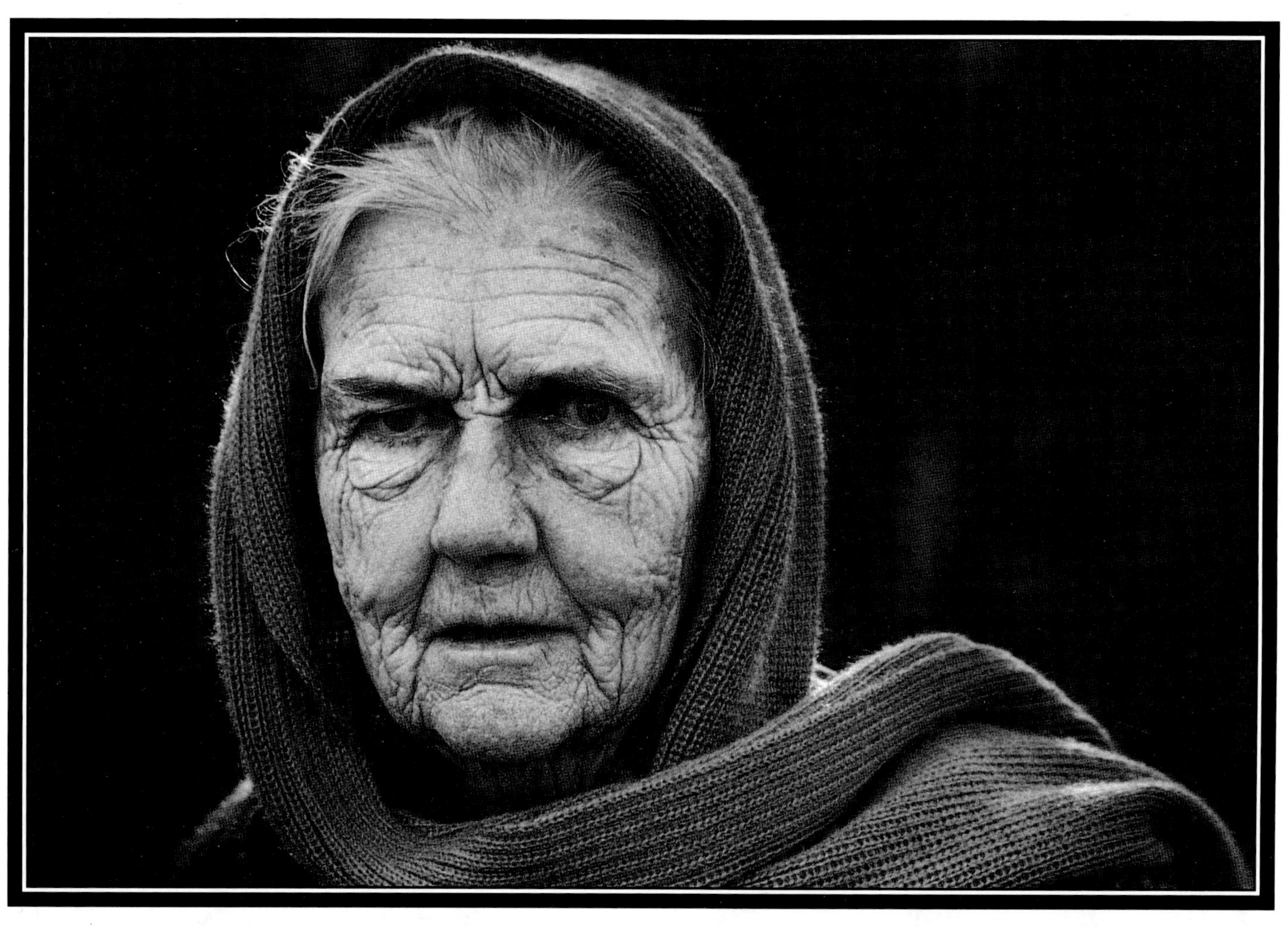

24.
The Octogenarian

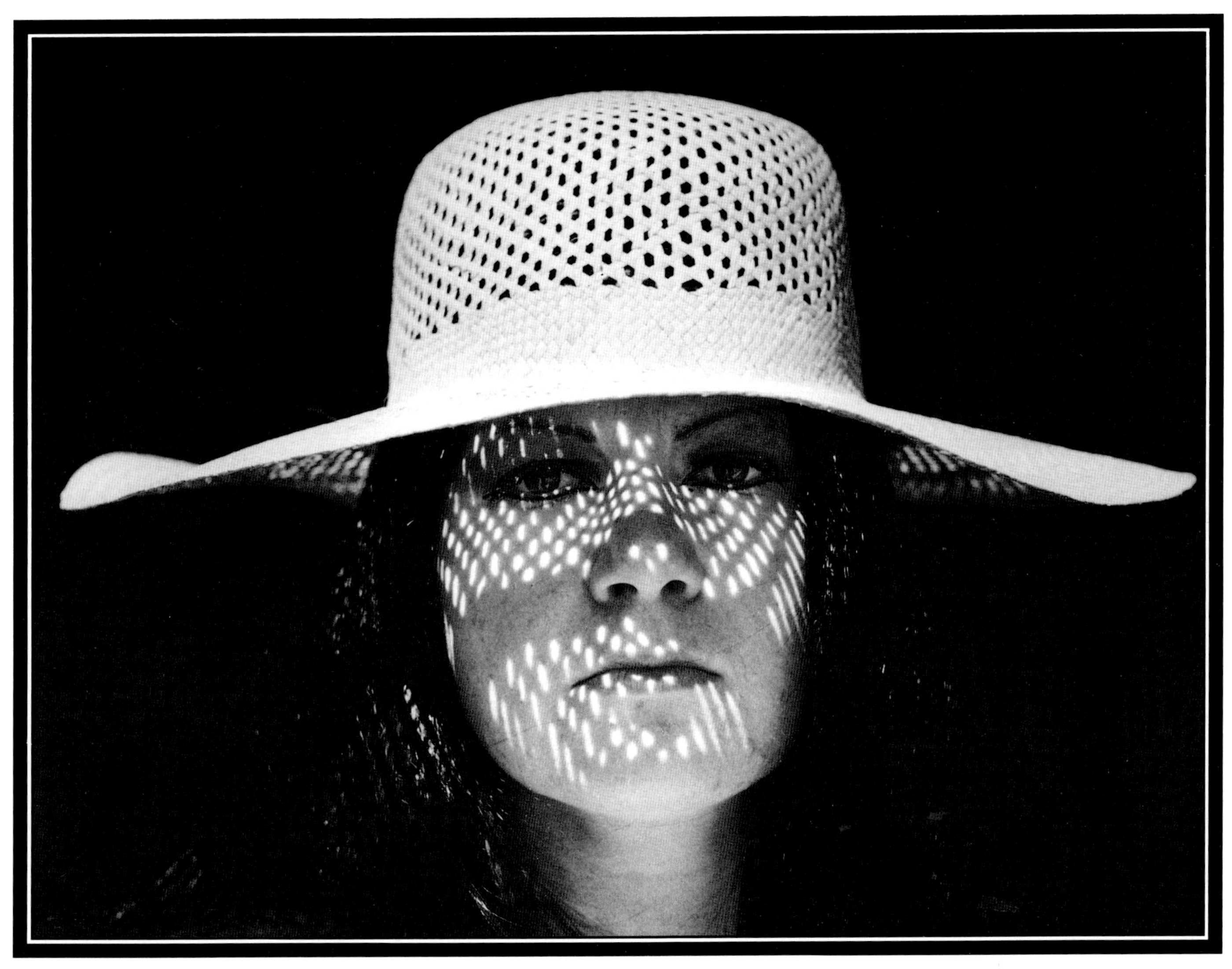

25.
The hat

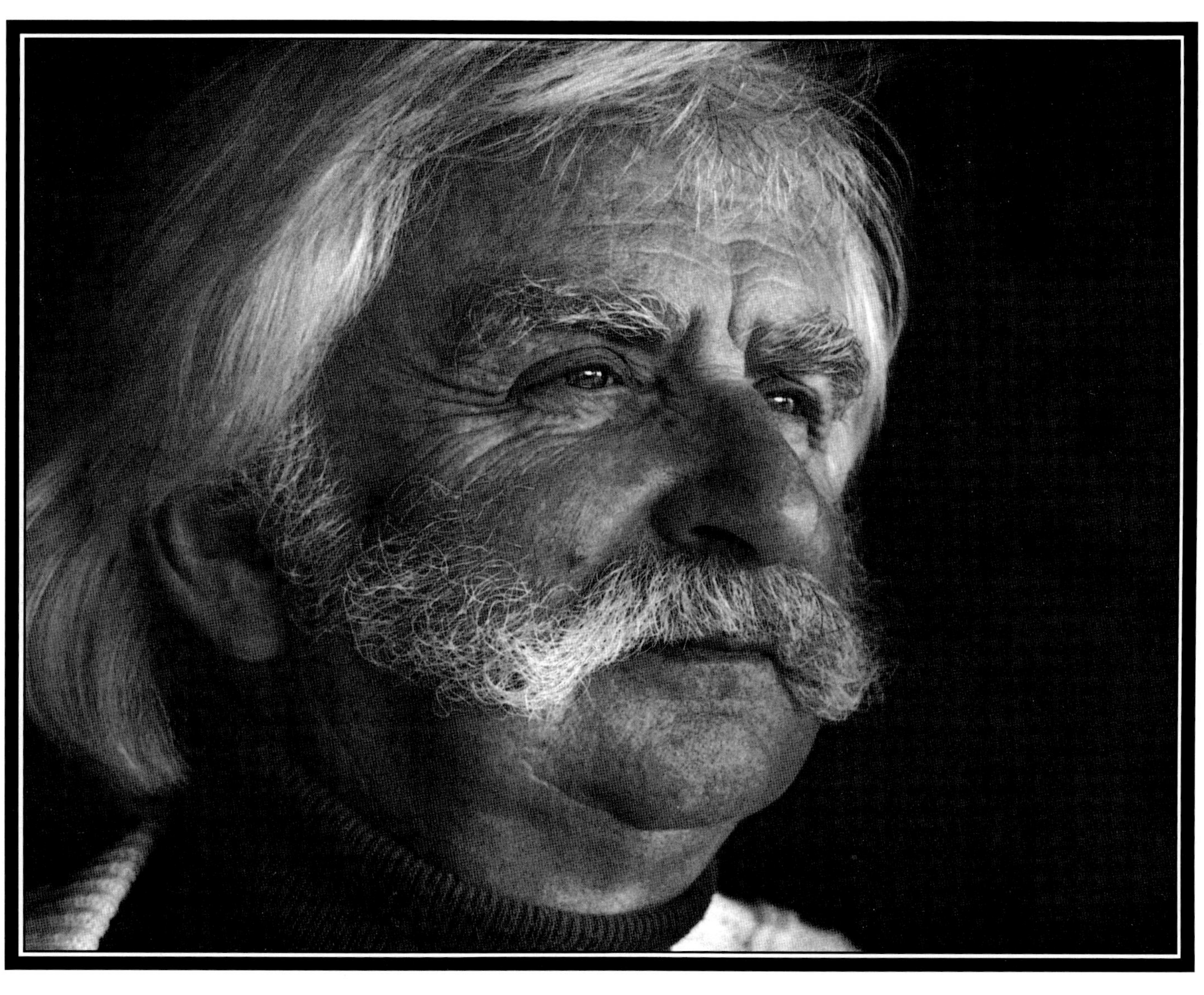

26.
Ron Baker
Lyme Regis, 1993

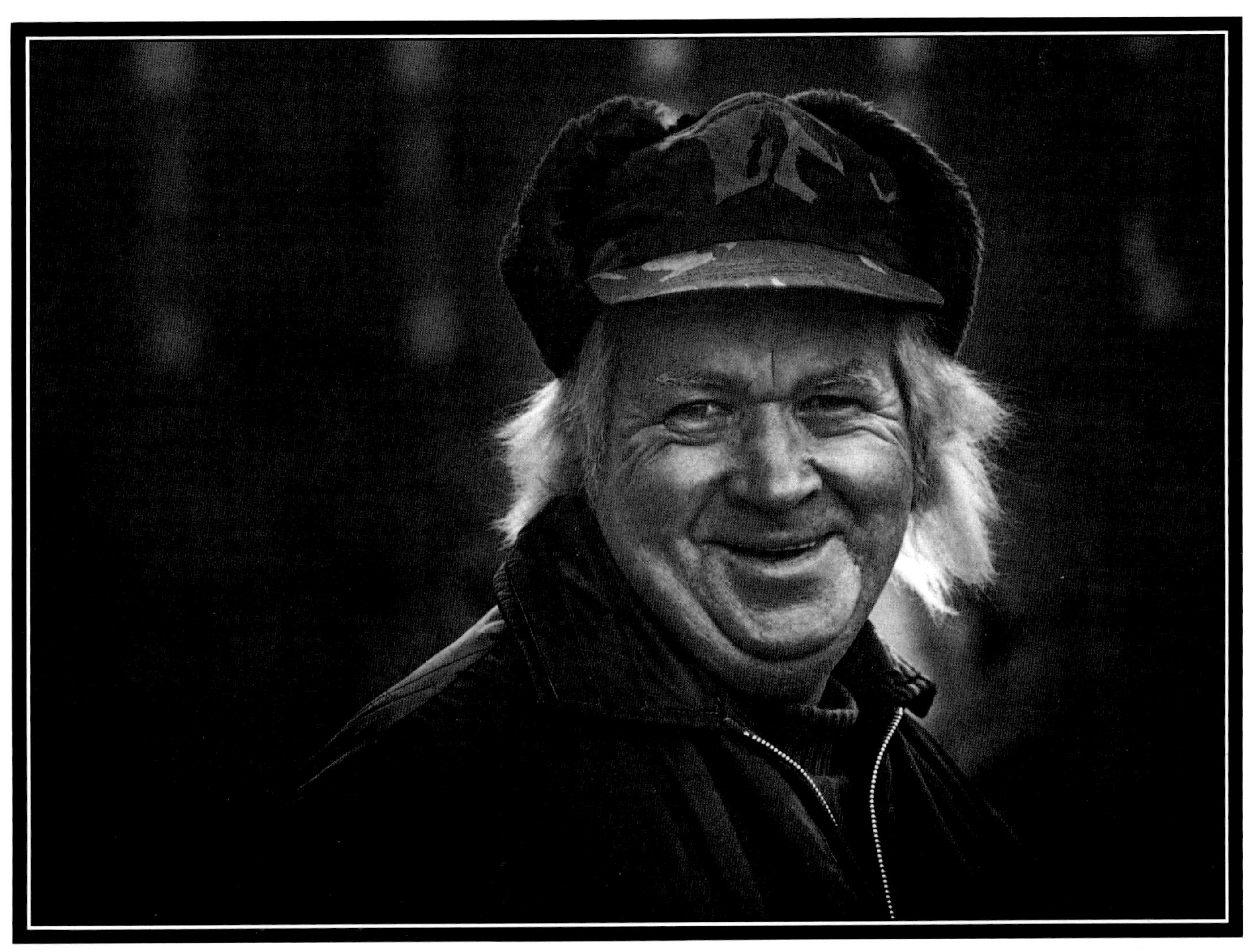

27.
Roger Gardener
Ordnance Survey, 1989

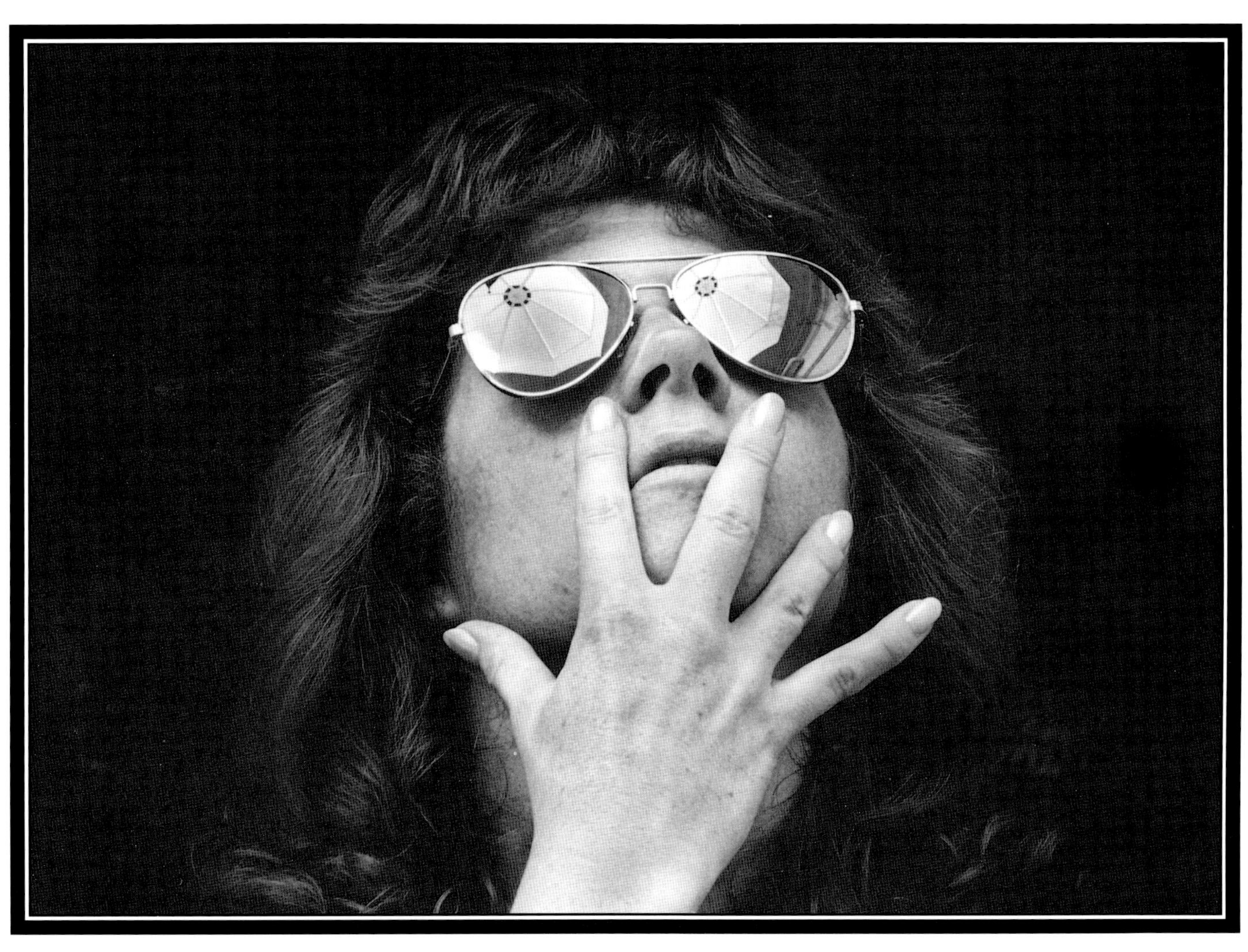

28.
Googly eyes

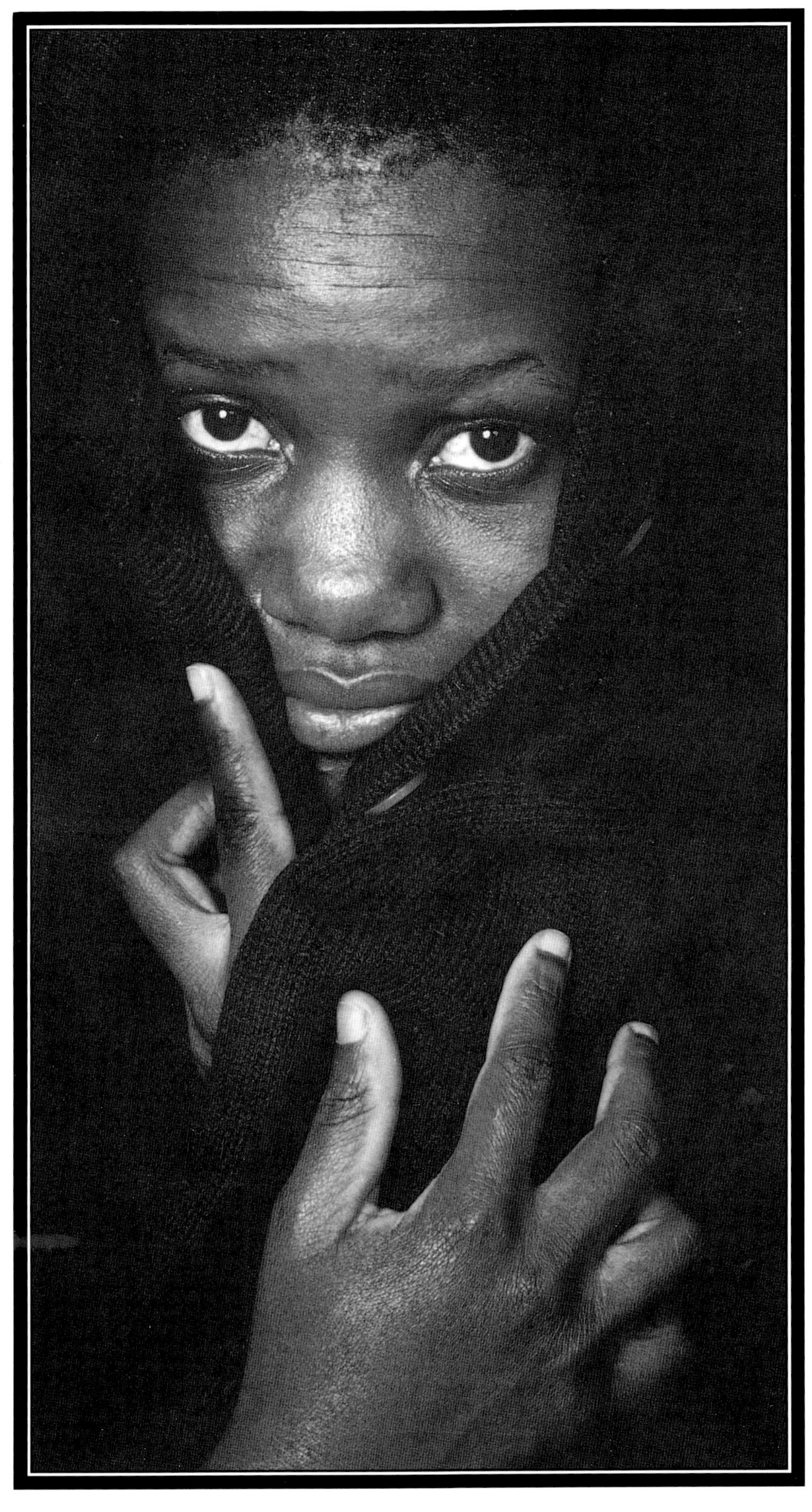

29.
Gertrude

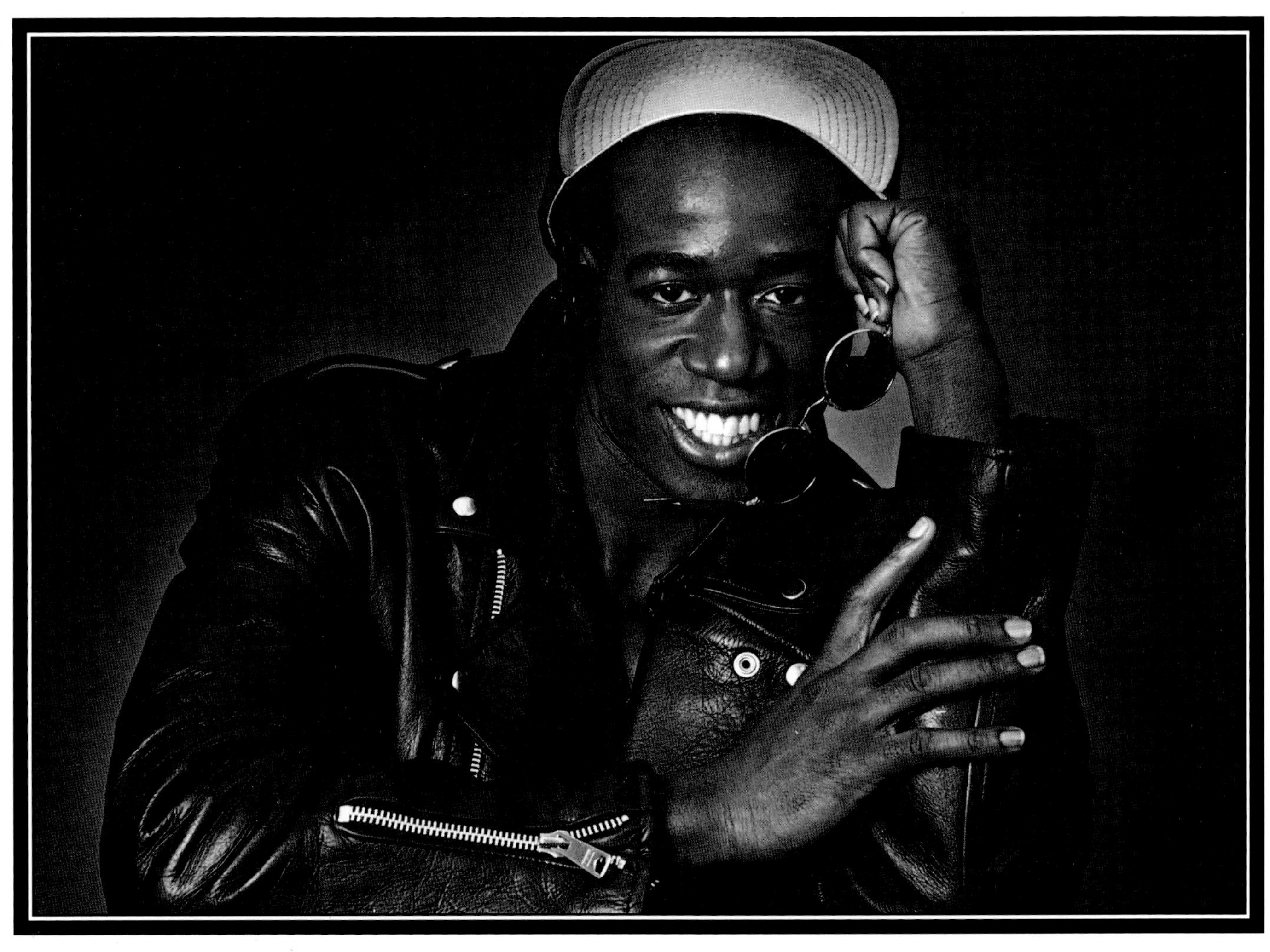

30.
The leather jacket

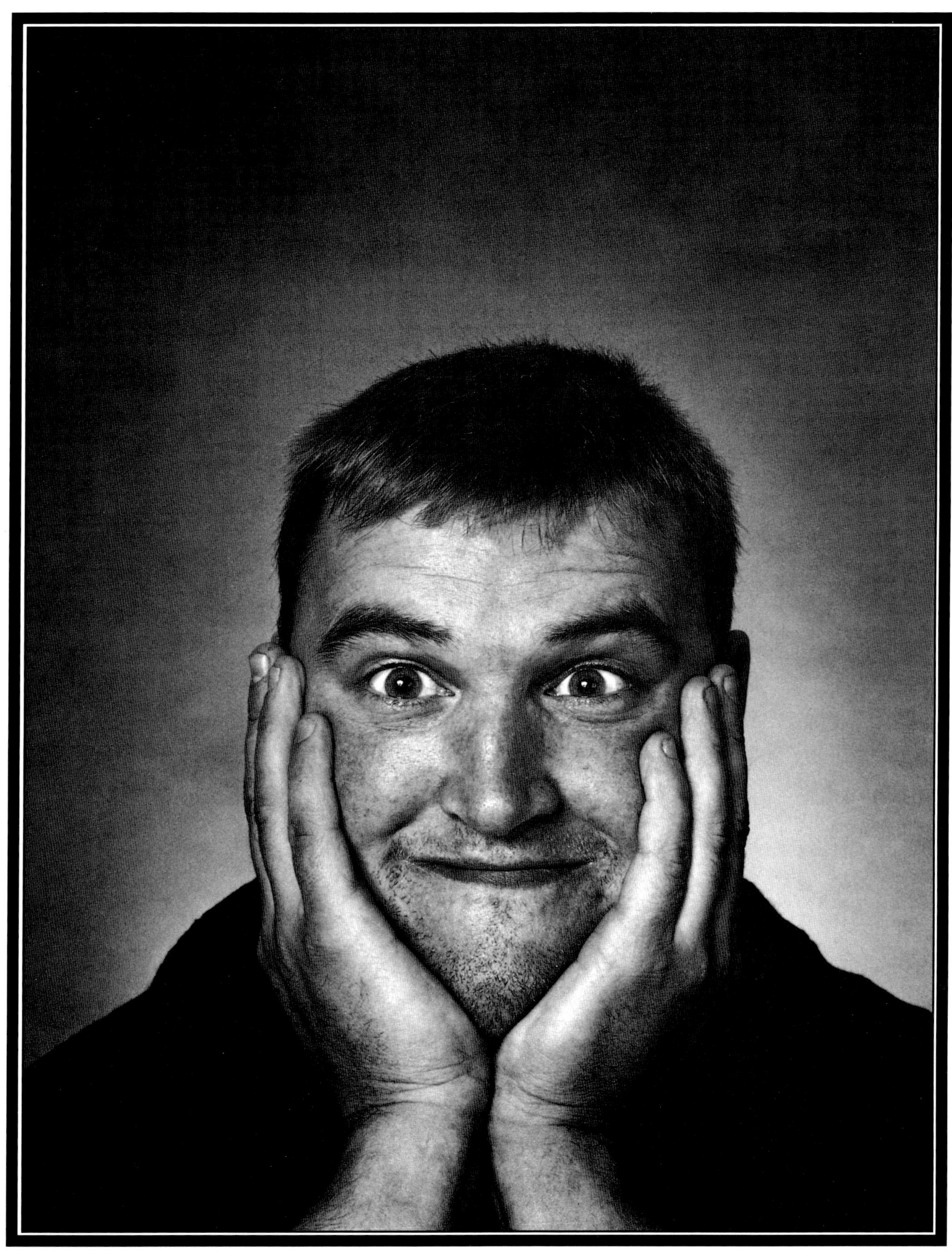

31.
Mike Bichard

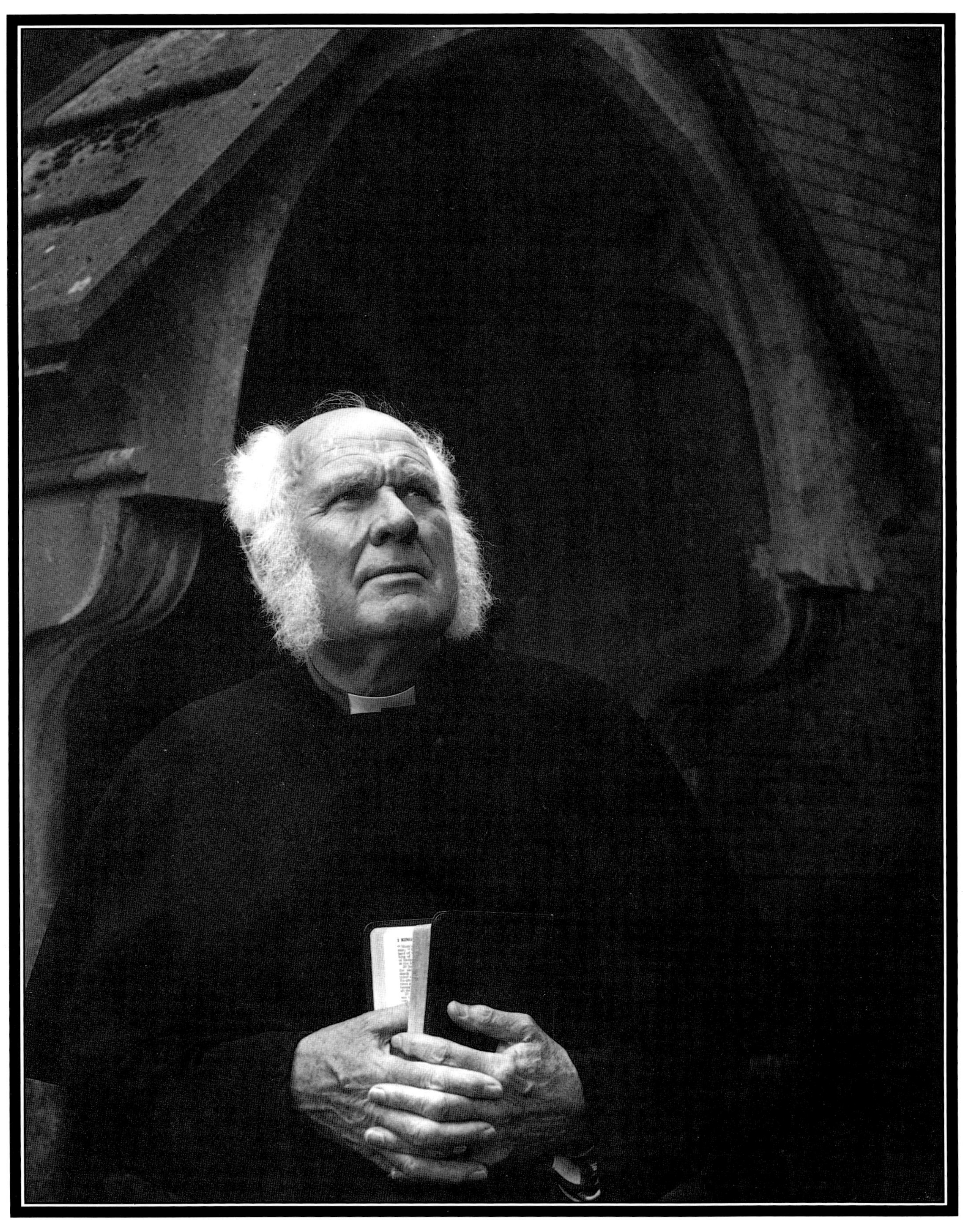

32.
Reverend Father Bianci

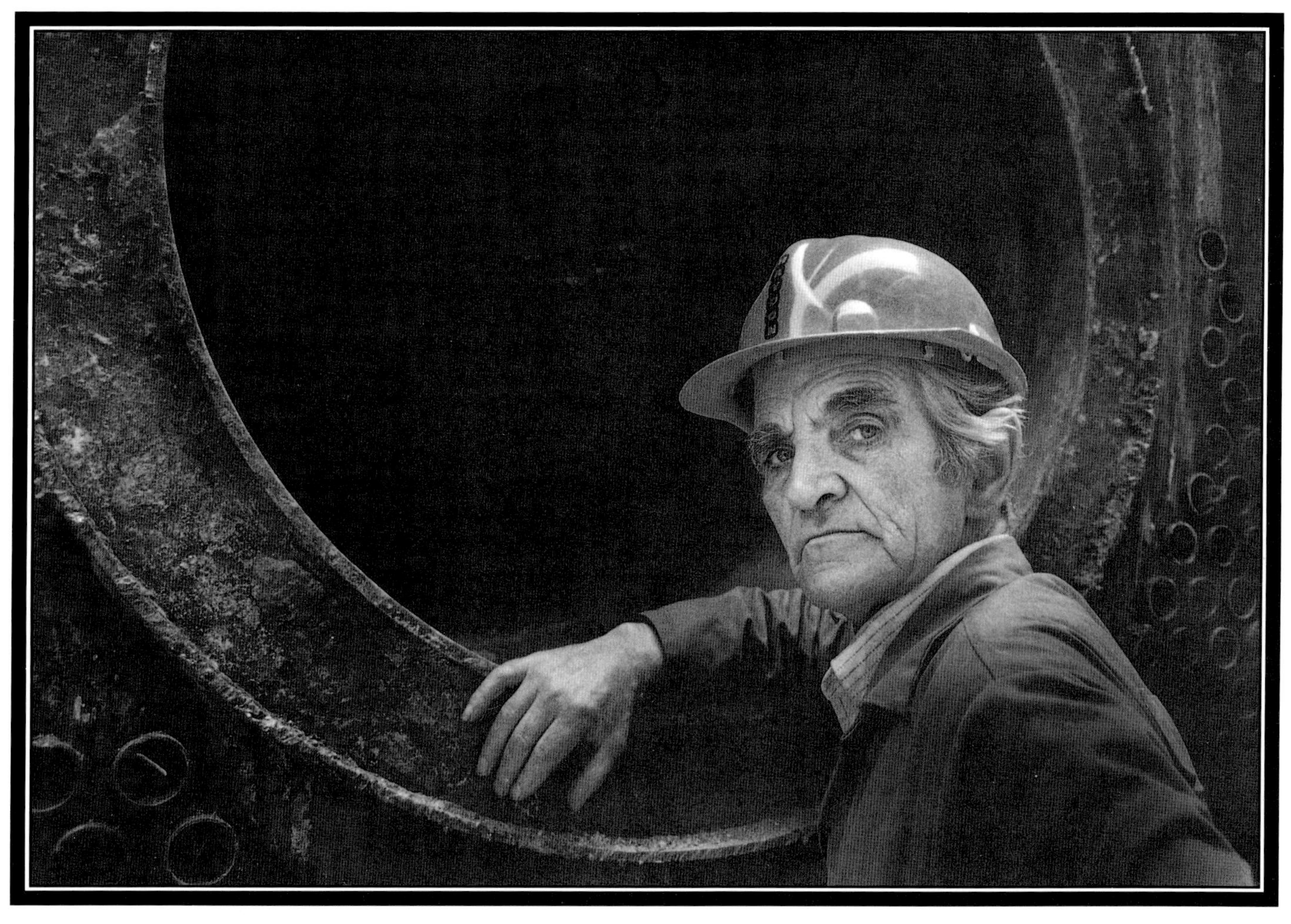

33.
The boilerman
Ordnance Survey, 1986

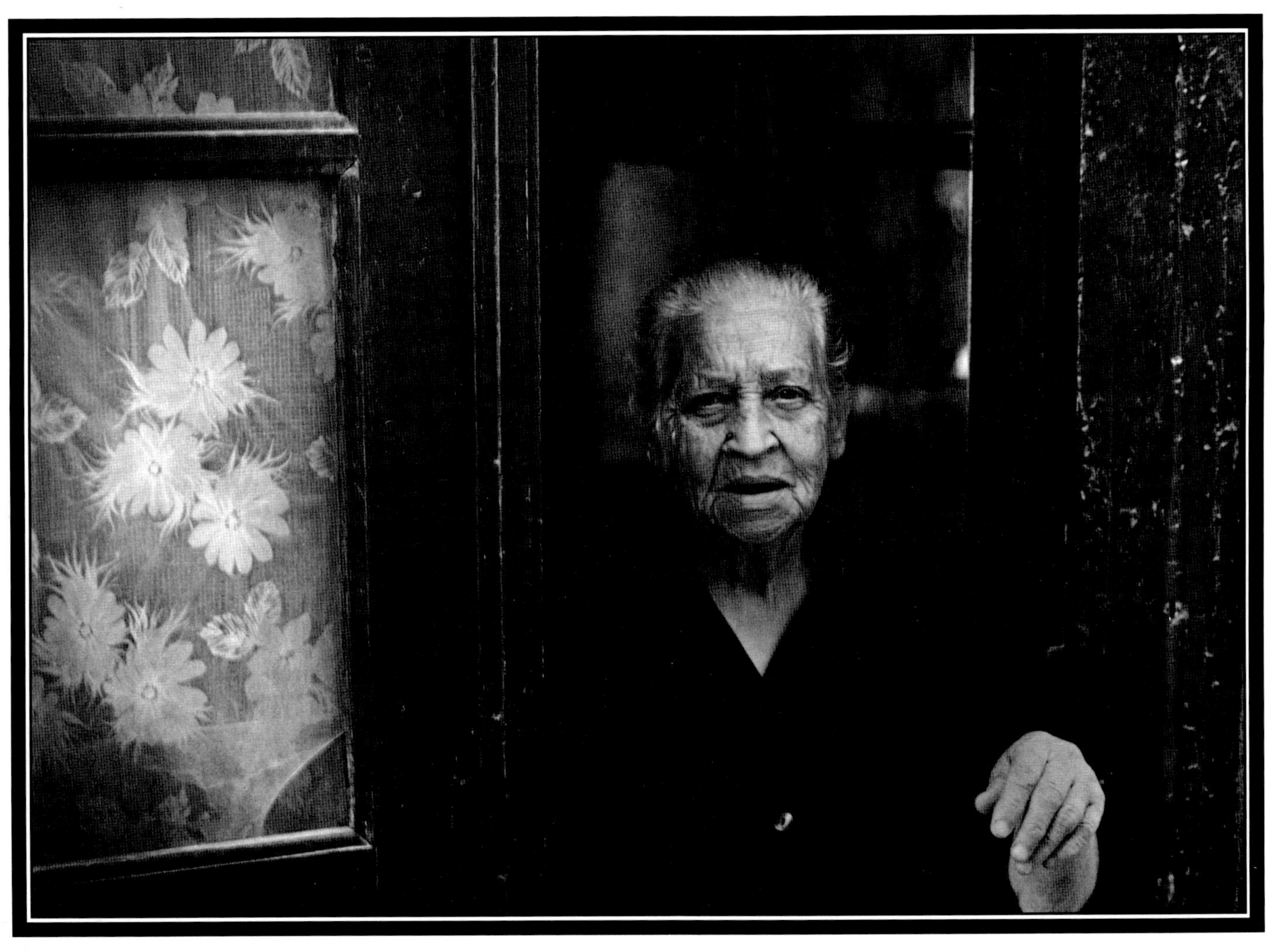

34.
Greek lady

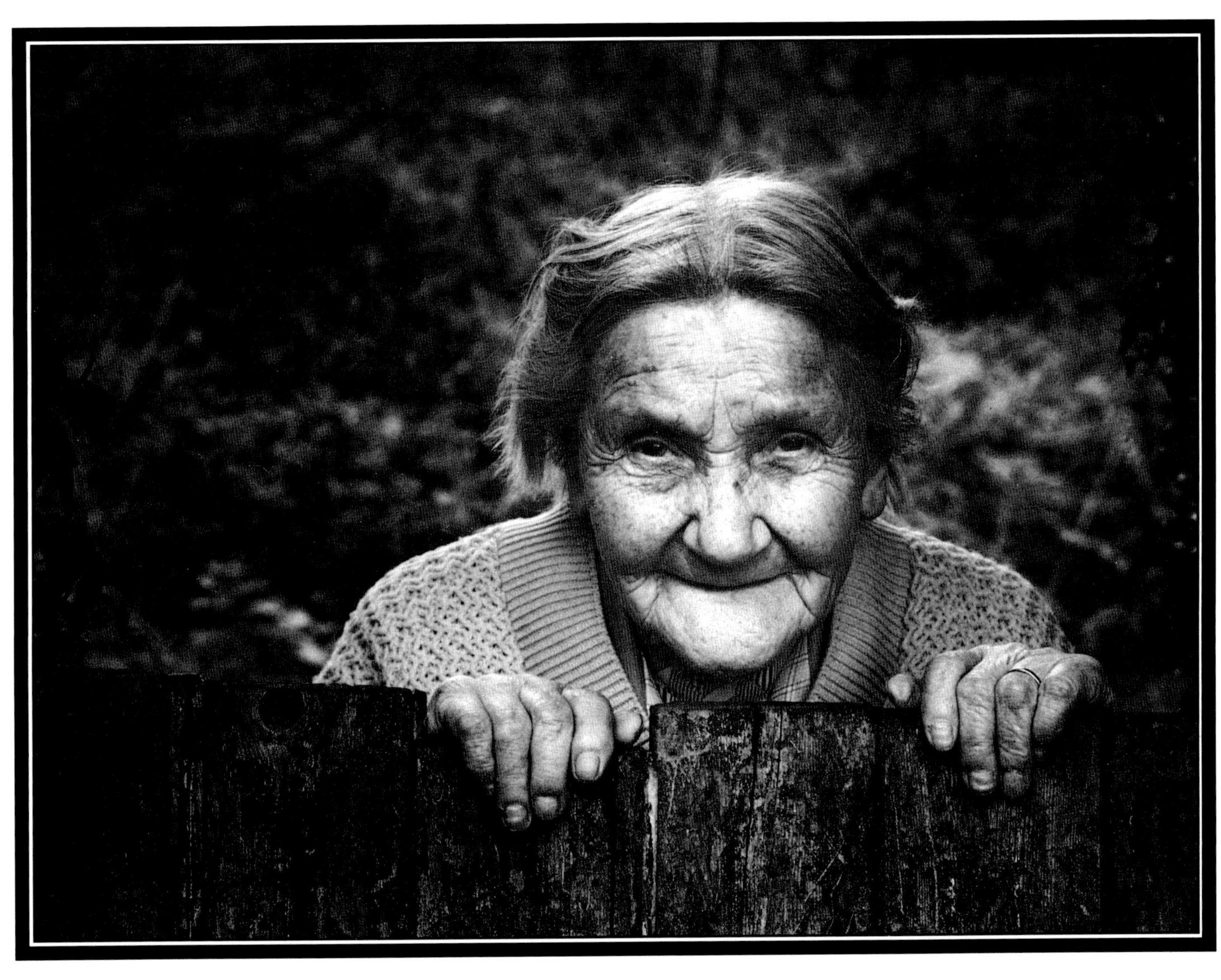

35.
Next door neighbour

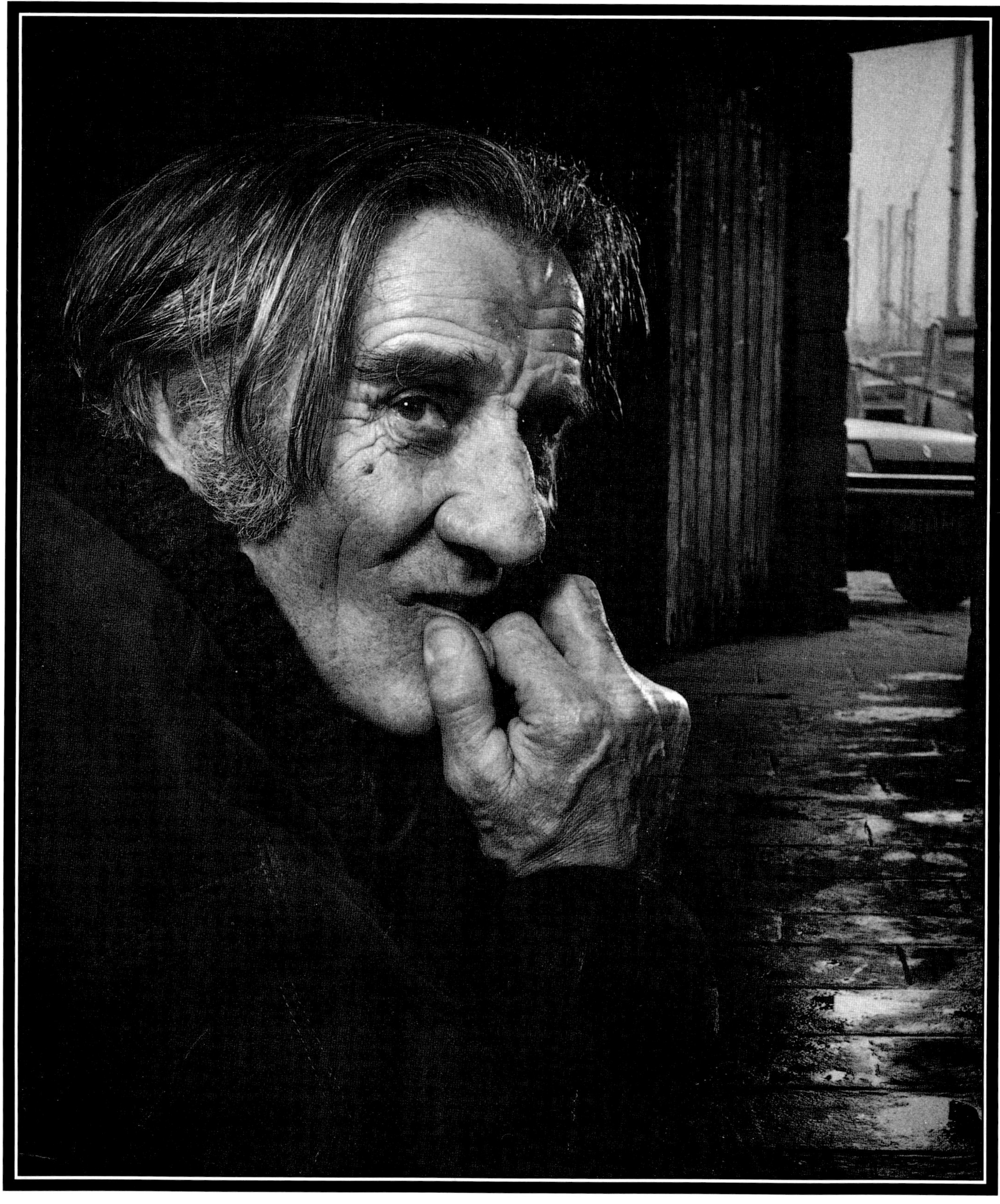

36.
Old salt

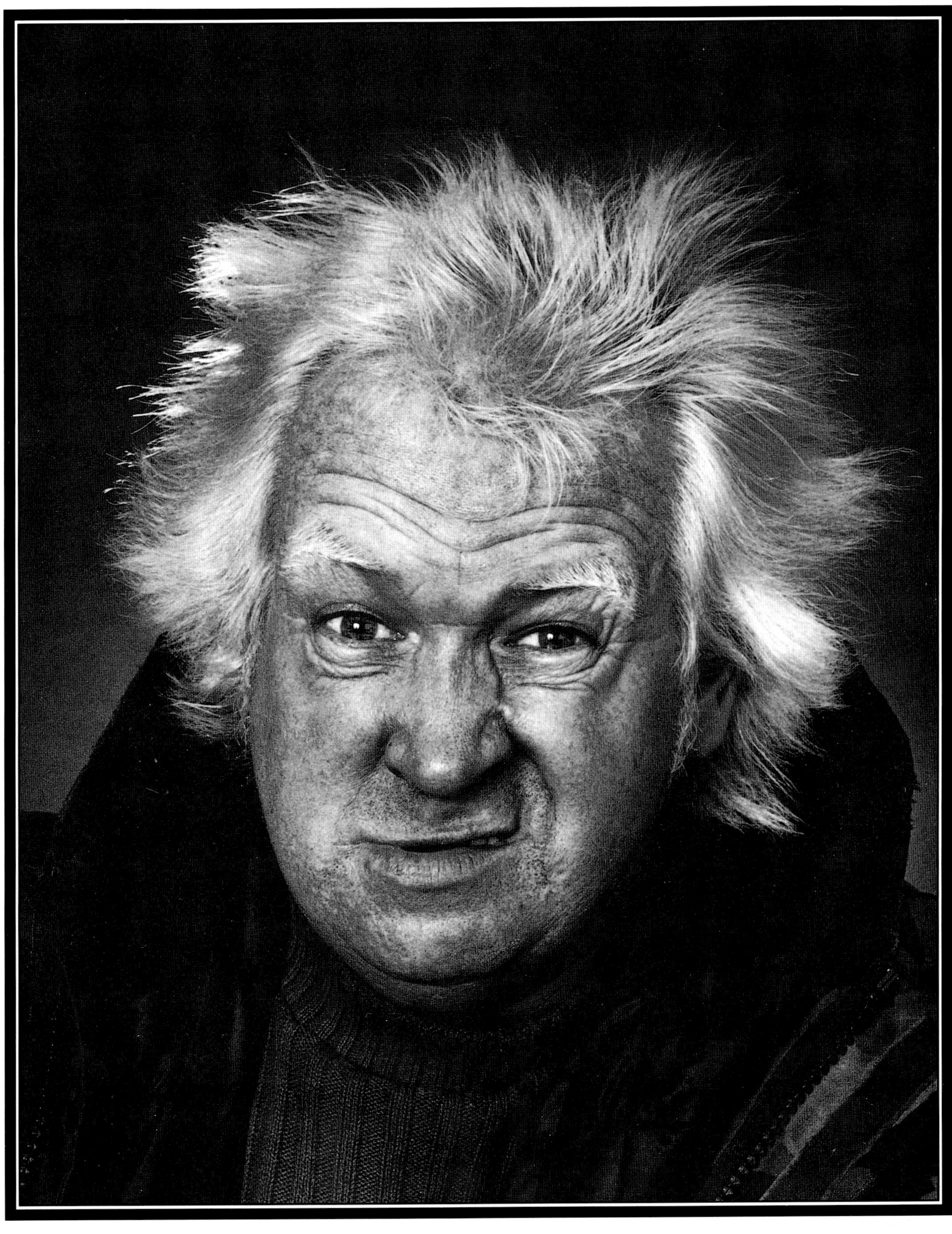

37.
Hair-do

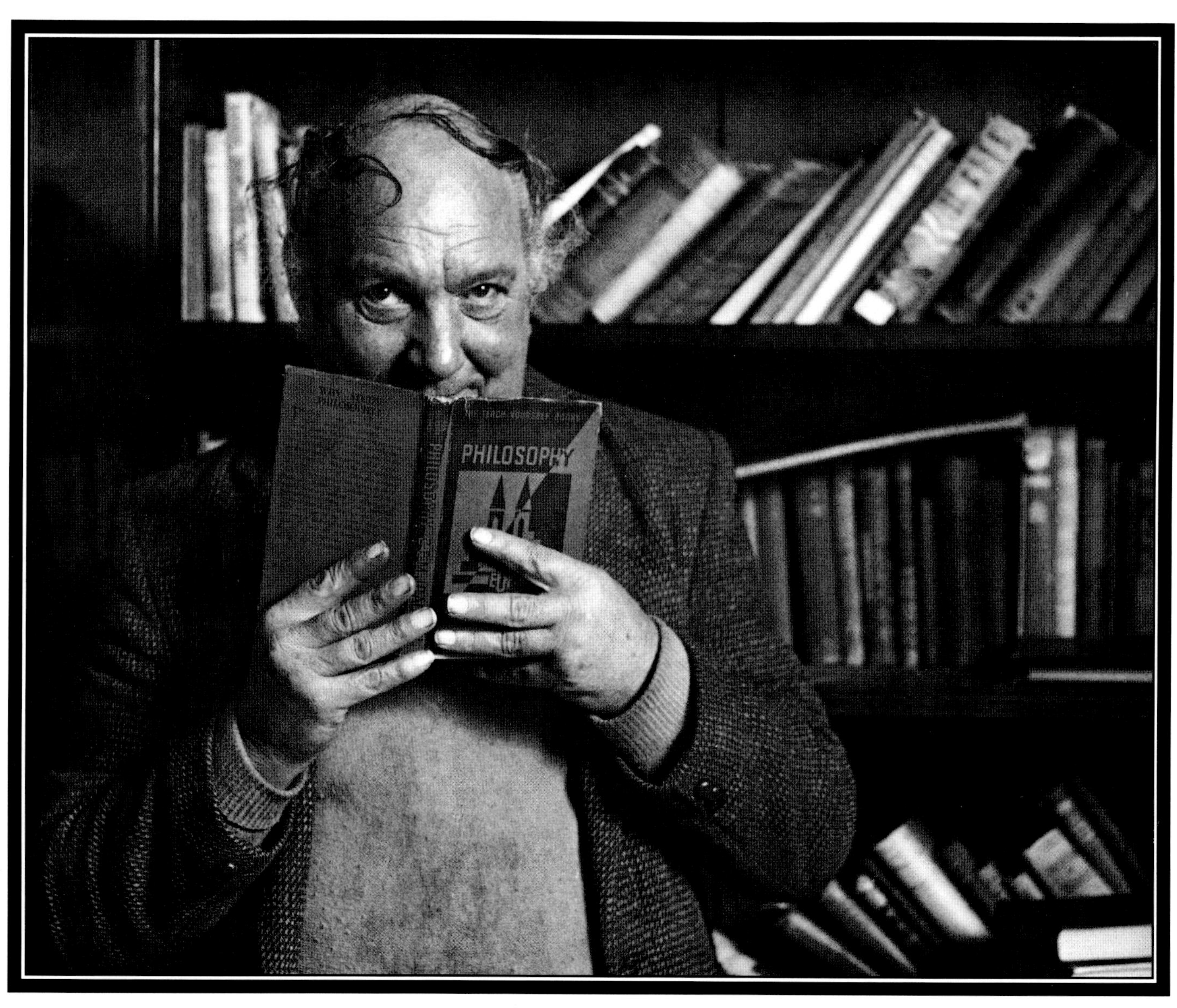

38.
The philosopher

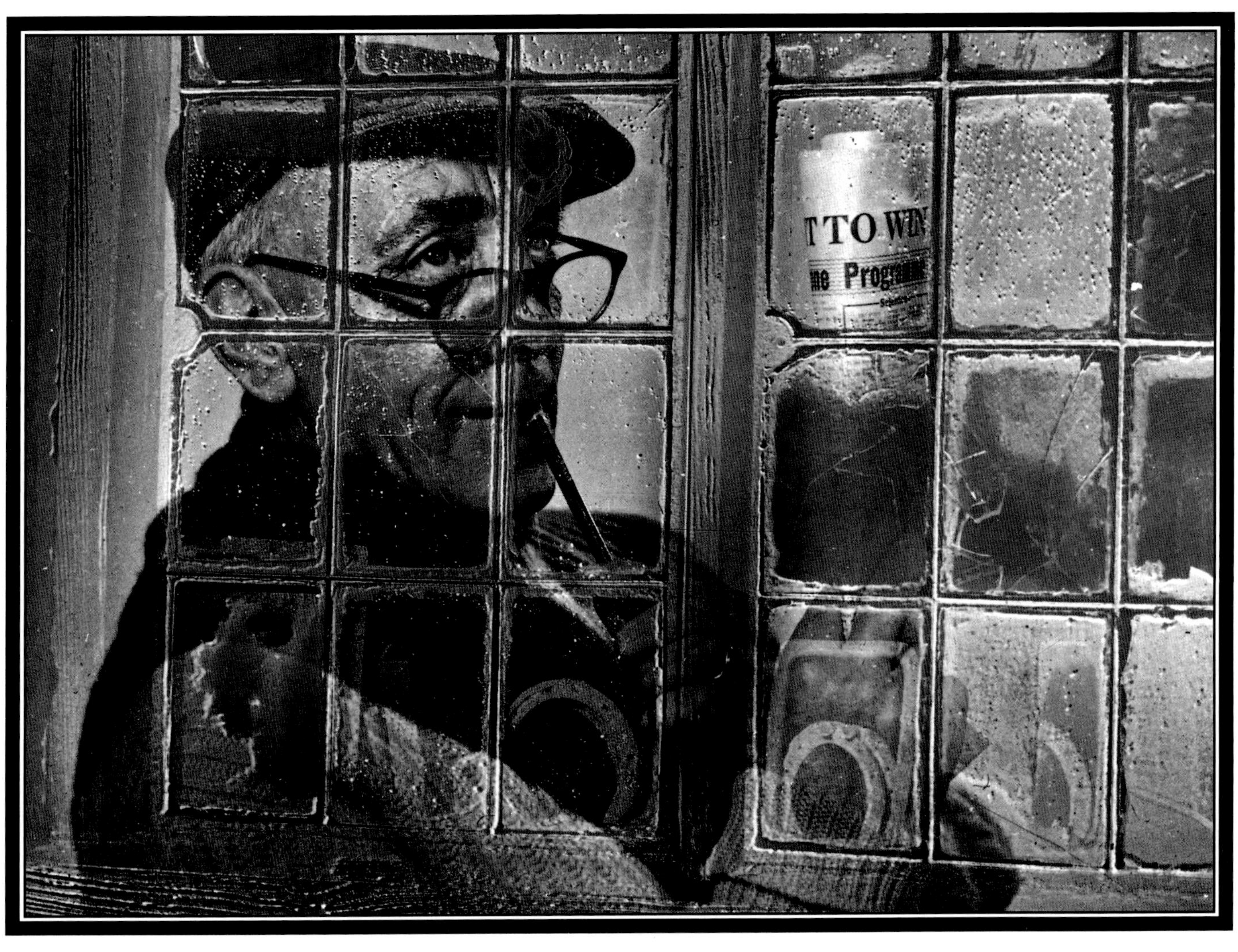

39.
Dreaming of a winner

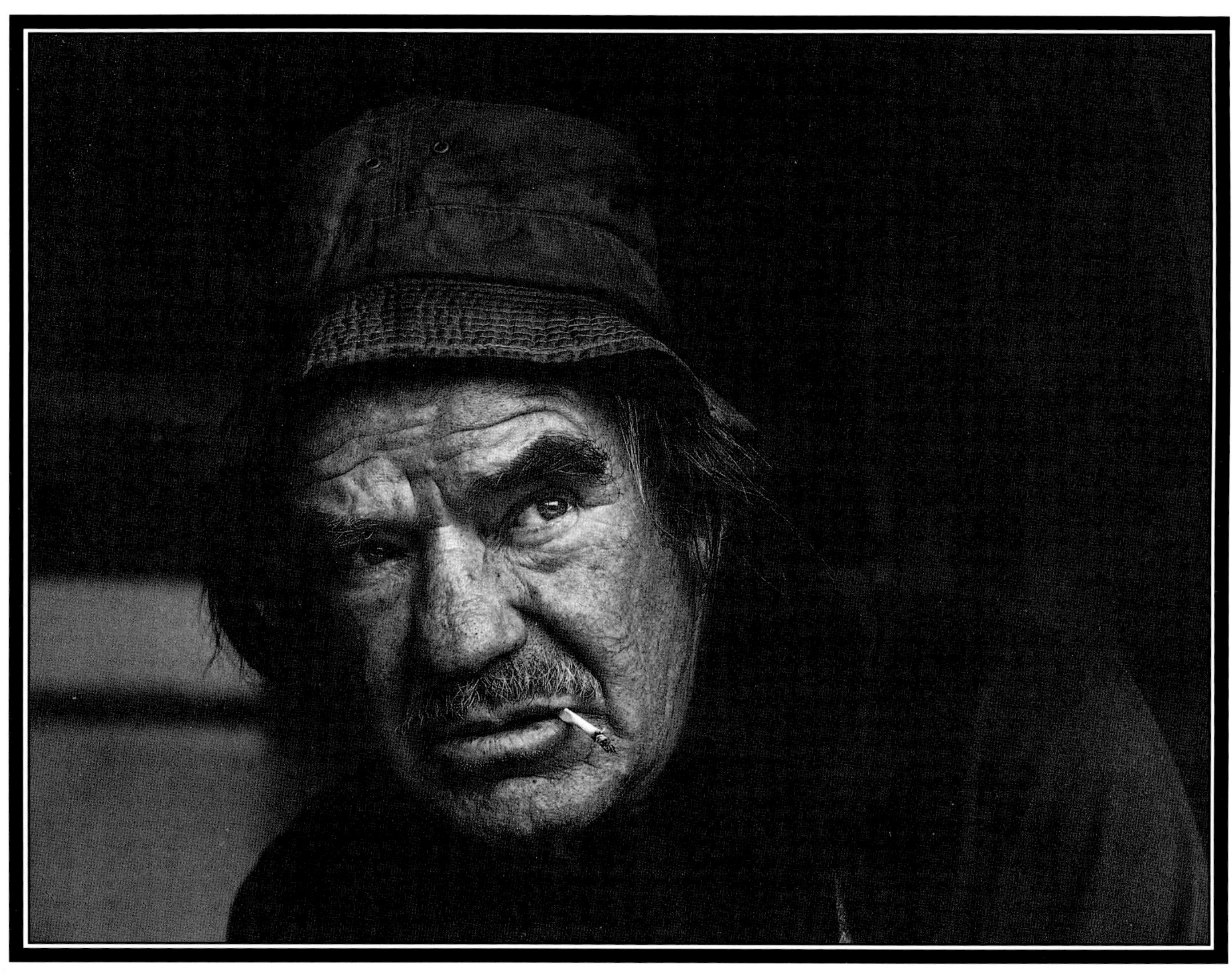

40.
Bob

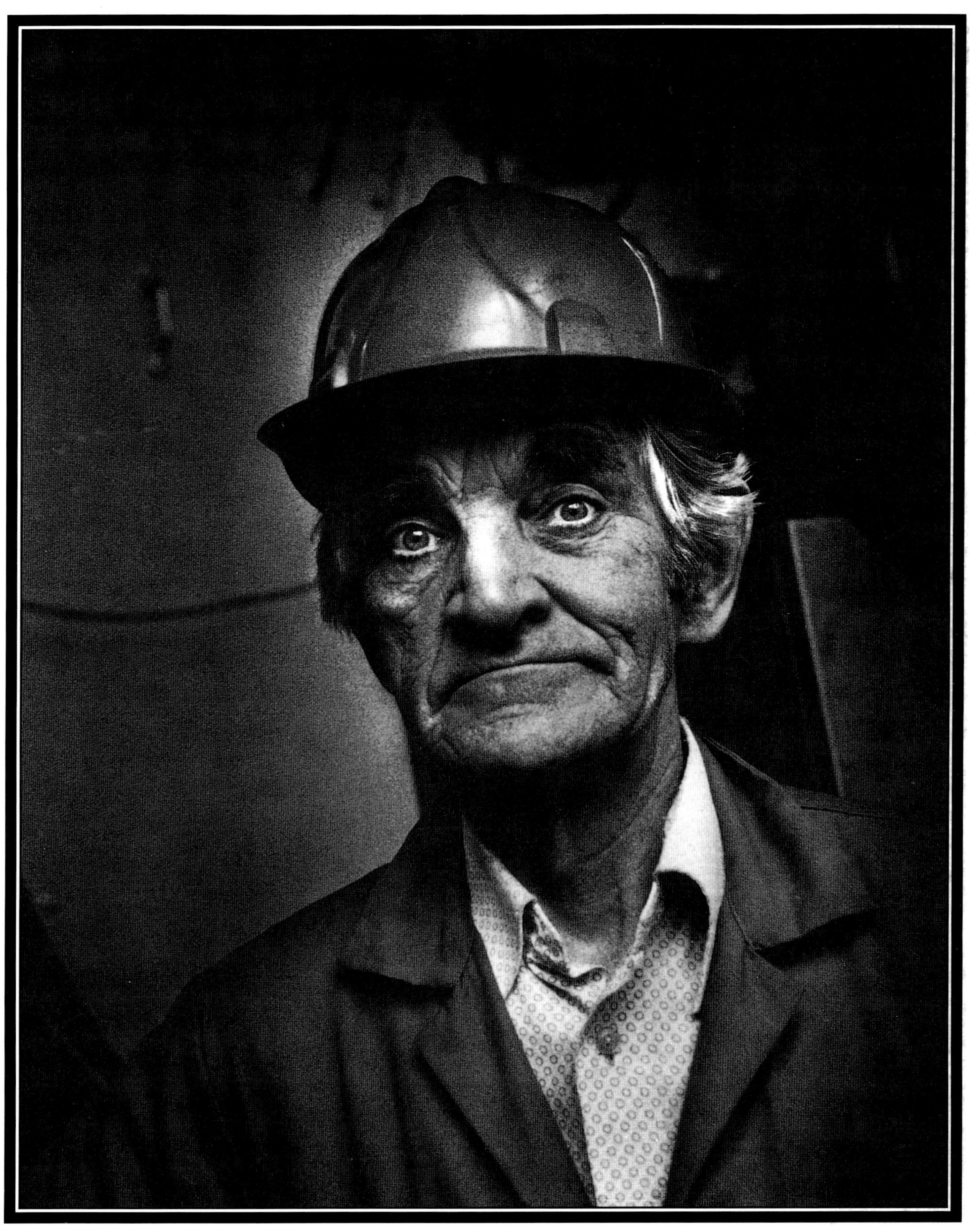

41.
Boilerman II
Ordnance Survey, 1986

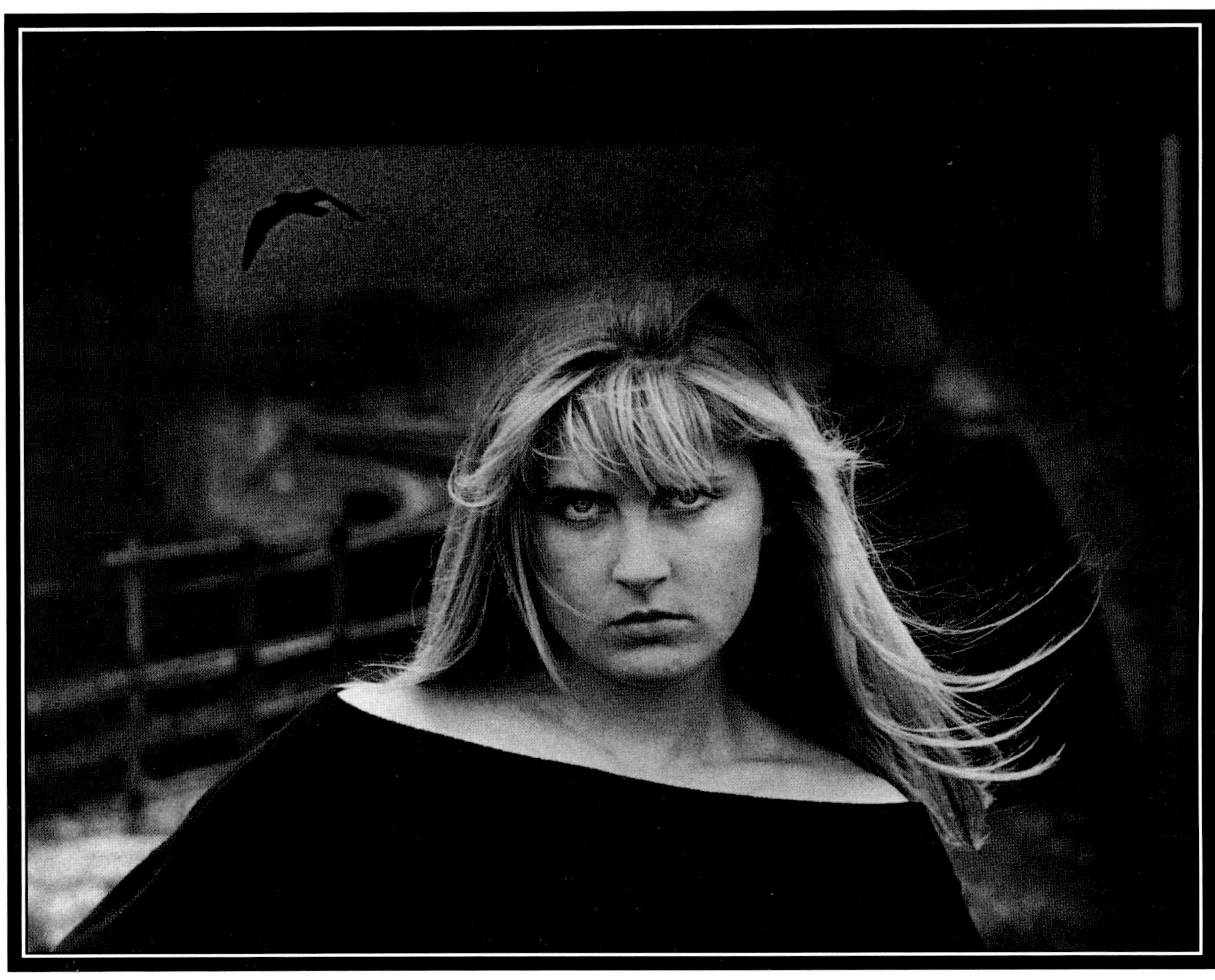

42.
Sophie

For further details of the Contemporary Portfolio Series and a catalogue of Creative Monochrome publications, please write to Creative Monochrome, 20 St Peters Road, Croydon, Surrey, CR0 1HD.